Advanced Pathf

Tests and tar

Other titles in the series

Developing learning strategies (APF2)
Barry Jones

Advancing oral skills (APF1)
Anneli McLachlan

Centre for Information
on Language Teaching and Research

The Centre for Information on Language Teaching and Research provides a complete range of services for language professionals in every stage and sector of education, and in business, in support of its brief to promote Britain's foreign language capability.

CILT is a registered charity, supported by Central Government grants. CILT is based in Covent Garden, London, and its services are delivered through a national collaborative network of regional Comenius Centres in England, the National Comenius Centre of Wales, Scottish CILT and Northern Ireland CILT.

advAnced
Pathfinder
3

Test and targets

TED NEATHER
WITH SOPHIE STRINGER-LAMARRE

CiLT
—— Centre for Information
on Language Teaching and Research

The views expressed in this publication are the authors' and do not necessarily represent those of CILT.

First published 2001 by the Centre for Information on Language Teaching and Research (CILT), 20 Bedfordbury, London WC2N 4LB

ISBN 1 902031 76 8

2005 2004 2003 2002 2001 / 10 9 8 7 6 5 4 3 2 1

A catalogue record for this book is available from the British Library

Printed in Great Britain by Copyprint UK Ltd

CILT Publications are available from: **Central Books,** 99 Wallis Rd, London E9 5LN. Tel: 020 8986 4854. Fax: 020 8533 5821. Book trade representation (UK and Ireland): **Broadcast Book Services,** Charter House, 27a London Road, Croydon CR0 2RE. Tel: 020 8681 8949. Fax: 020 8688 0615.

Acknowledgements

My particular thanks go to Ian Maun for fruitful discussions on text difficulty, and to Emma Rees for the sympathetic way she has of coaxing an author in the direction he should go.

A particular vote of thanks goes to Sophie Stringer-Lamarre for contributing her chapter on vocational qualifications.

Exam Boards and addresses

AQA
Stag Hill House, Guildford,
Surrey GU2 5XJ
Tel: 01483 506 506
Fax: 01483 300 152
Website: www.aeb.org.uk

City and Guilds
Under the umbrella of AQA
1 Giltspur Street,
London EC1A 9DD
Tel: 020 7294 2800/1/2
Fax: 020 7294 2400
Website: www.city-and-guilds.co.uk

Edexcel
Stewart House, 32 Russell
Square, London, WC1B 5DN
Tel: 0870 240 9800
Fax: 020 7758 6960
Website: www.edexcel.org.uk

LCCI Examinations Board
Athena House, 112 Station Road,
Sidcup DA15 7BJ
Tel: 020 8302 0261
Fax: 020 8302 4169
Website: www.lccieb.org.uk/lccieb

Northern Ireland Council for the Curriculum, Examinations and Assessment (CCEA)
Clarendon Dock, 29 Clarendon
Road, Belfast BT1 3BG
Tel: 028 9026 1200
Fax: 028 9026 1234
Website: www.ccea.org.uk

OCR
1 Regent Street,
Cambridge CB2 1GG
Tel: 01223 552 552
Fax: 01223 552 553
Website: www.ocr.org.uk

Welsh Joint Education Committee (WJEC)
245 Western Avenue,
Cardiff CF5 2YX
Tel: 029 2026 5000
Fax: 029 2057 5894
Website: www.wjec.co.uk

Introduction

The aims of this book

This book sets out to describe the current position with regard to post-GCSE testing in Modern Foreign Languages (MFL). The field covered is therefore both the new A level (AS/A2) and also developments in the vocational sector. Chapters 1 and 2 provide the background necessary to set recent developments into a proper context. Chapters 3, 4 and 5 deal with changes in examination requirements. The central concern is the effect on teachers of such changes and the ways in which classroom methods have been adapted. Chapter 6 focuses specifically on the implications for teaching methods of the new criteria. However, the point is strongly made, that the most recent syllabus changes do not require major changes in teaching methods, although there is a need for some adaptations to the new framework and the style of exam tasks. The good practice which teachers have built up in recent years in their approach to target-language teaching, working with authentic texts and developing all skills equally, remain as valid for the new schemes of work as they were previously. Chapter 7 provides the background to the current range of vocational qualifications and a discussion of the advantages of such qualifications.

Choosing a path through the book

The chapters of the book are, to some extent, self-contained. It is not necessary to work through the book systematically from Chapter 1. The following section gives a more detailed overview of the content of chapters, so that readers may plan their own course through the book according to their interests. Each chapter concludes with a short summary of key points.

Chapter 1: Teachers who remember the days when A level examinations were traditionally concerned with translation and the study of literary texts may sometimes feel a whiff of nostalgia and seek to remind themselves how exactly the changes have taken place over the years. For teachers who have entered the profession in recent years, it may seem that A level teaching of foreign languages is subject to constant flux and change. They may sometimes ask themselves where the impetus for such changes comes from and by what paths we have arrived at the current position where they teach not only a whole range of language skills but also focus on a bewildering variety of contemporary issues and topics. To respond to all such queries, Chapter 1 provides some historical background to the current proposals, showing how thinking has evolved over the period. Important issues are raised, such as the comparability of demand between Exam Boards. The frequent lament that standards have fallen is addressed and put into the context of current demands on students.

Chapter 2 focuses on the developments leading directly to the Dearing Report of 1996 and the new pattern of AS/A2 examinations.

Chapter 3 offers a description and discussion of the main features of the new specifications.

Chapter 4 extends the debate on key issues: the nature of authenticity; the place of grammar in a teaching and testing programme; the pros and cons of a topic-based approach; definitions of text difficulty; the differing demands made by certain test-types. It is often the case that key concepts, such as authenticity or target-language teaching, become so much the accepted wisdom of the day that their meaning and wider significance is no longer a subject for debate. This chapter deliberately focuses on such areas and seeks to inform teachers of the issues.

Chapter 5 offers a detailed examination of examination tasks and test-types, as they have been presented by the Boards in the specimen papers for French at AS/A2. (There is some reference also to the first AS papers set by OCR in January 2001).

Chapter 6 takes up the points raised by the structure of the new examination (Chapter 3) and the examination requirements (Chapter 5) and explores the implications for teaching. Further advice, help and information are given by other books in the CILT *Advanced Pathfinder* series.

Chapter 7 offers an account of another area of growing significance: vocational language teaching and testing. The background to the vocational sector is presented and a selection of available qualifications discussed. New vocational qualifications are presented with a discussion of their advantages and the motivation they offer to students.

1

Shifting targets

Aims

The aim of this chapter is to establish the historical context within which the new AS/A2 syllabuses and the GNVQ plans are being proposed. How has the philosophy of language testing changed over the last twenty years? What are the changing demands of examination criteria? The information in this chapter outlines a context which will enable readers better to evaluate and understand the current situation.

Changes at A level 1977–1998

The transformation in the national organisation of examinations since the late 70s has been quite radical. Mergers have reduced the eight Boards setting A level exams to five, of which two, the Northern Ireland Board (CCEA) and the Welsh Board (WJEC) are largely regional. With regard specifically to Modern Foreign Languages, syllabuses have developed from a document of barely more than a page in length (e.g. London 1977) to detailed specifications of 119 pages (e.g. Edexcel 2000).

Such changes at A level in Modern Foreign Languages (MFL) between 1977 and 1998 reflect changing attitudes both to the nature of foreign language study and the style of foreign language testing. The aim of language study has increasingly been seen as communication in the widest sense, and therefore, the concern of an A level course was to develop all the language skills – speaking and listening as well as reading and writing. Following on from those developments, language testing became more concerned to assess the full range of language skills, both receptive and productive, and to base that assessment on authentic materials, closely related to issues in contemporary society.

All Boards have provided an increasing range of detailed information over the years. The 1977 syllabus specified little more than the names of examination papers and their duration. Most space was taken up with a list of set texts. By 1997, the practices of the examination and its underlying philosophy were made clear. Although the philosophy and aims of syllabuses were not stated in 1976/7, it seems clear from syllabus content, question papers and mark-schemes that the A level examinations in MFL were intended to assess candidates' suitability for a traditional degree course. One major requirement was detailed knowledge and understanding of literary works. The other was competence in translating, from and into the foreign language, difficult and unpredictable texts, usually extracts from 19th and 20th century novels. But sixth forms and universities were changing as their student population changed. Over the period 1962/3 to 1997/8, the numbers of students going on to Higher Education rose from 216,000 to 1.2 million, i.e. more than 30% of the age-group (*National statistics: Social trends,* 2000, pp54–55). Sixth forms and other post-16 classes increasingly had to meet the needs of a more varied body of students, covering a wider spread of ability and often combining their language study with other, non-language subjects. So there were movements towards making language examinations more 'accessible', more 'relevant', with a wider range of more practical applications.

The introduction of GCSE in 1988 was undoubtedly the major factor in changing the focus of language courses and assessment. Candidates entering upon A level courses after this date had a quite different background of preparation from that provided by O level. What is quite clear from all these developments, is the powerful 'backwash' effect of examinations upon teaching programmes and methods. For example, if the proportion of marks given for oral performance rises from under 10% to over 25%, it is inevitable that oral activities will become more of a priority in classroom activities. This effect will be further discussed among the issues raised in Chapter 4.

Major syllabus changes

Since 1976/7, the major changes have been concentrated in three main areas: the content of syllabuses, the weighting of components and the approach to constructing mark-schemes. Concerning content, there has never been, at A level, a language content defined in terms of lexis and structures, such as was introduced for GCSE in 1988. A level language content was established, in more traditional syllabuses, by the largely literary register of the passages chosen for translation. In current syllabuses, there has been a shift away from that register and content is now established by the range of authentic language presented in the texts of the examination and by the linguistically imprecise framework of topics. (At GCSE, topics are organised within the even broader categories of Areas of Experience.) One evident result of these changes of approach is that examination papers have become more interesting in their layout, with a more 'authentic' appearance. The concern for authenticity of unedited texts and the resulting wide range of language was one reason for the introduction of dictionaries in examinations by some Boards.

Cultural content

As indicated above, the cultural content of syllabuses up to and including 1977 was defined almost exclusively in terms of the study of a small number of literary set-texts. Although literary studies in some form are still available as an option in all current syllabus specifications, they are no longer the only, compulsory form of cultural study. Cultural content has now been extended beyond the traditional, literary definition to allow breadth of choice across all aspects of contemporary society, starting with issues such as the family and patterns of daily life and moving out into areas of work and leisure, the media, the arts, the environment and the place of the language being studied in the international as well as national community. The main current concerns of paper setters choosing foreign language examination passages are their authenticity and contemporary relevance. Passages chosen therefore offer a far greater range and variety of register and subject matter. This range of subject matter has been further extended by the introduction of coursework options and by allowing more individual choice as to whether exam essays should be written on literary or non-literary topics.

Additional assessed skills

The introduction of additional assessed skills has, over time, most significantly affected the balance of assessment, and therefore also teaching approaches. Listening was not even tested by all Boards in 1976, whereas by 1998 Listening carried around 20% of marks, depending on the Board. The oral similarly moved to take 20% to 30% of marks. Translation from the foreign language into English had a much reduced role as a test and was supplemented by other tests of reading comprehension, often requiring the candidates to read longer passages for both detailed and gist comprehension. The assessment of productive writing changed so that there was a wider range of examination tasks than the prose translation and foreign language essay of previous years. Candidates up to and including the 2000 exam were actually required to write a great deal more than in the past. They also had to demonstrate a greater range of linguistic skills, such as are implied by mixed-skill tests which integrate listening and reading with writing in the foreign language.

The aim of all these developments has been parity between the language skills and the fostering of communication both receptive and productive, both spoken and written. It is important to note that today's candidates are faced, in all skill areas, with demands to demonstrate awareness of a much wider variety of styles and registers than was previously the case.

It is not only candidates who have such additional burdens. Teachers of foreign languages could once concentrate on a relatively limited range of skills and knowledge. One should not underestimate the increased demands made on sixth-form teachers by current examinations and specifications. Teachers now have to be fluent practitioners, able to use the target language in presenting and discussing a wide range of subjects. The knowledge and understanding of the very wide range of topics and issues they must address requires constant updating. It is no longer sufficient for teachers to be competent linguists. The requirements in terms of breadth of knowledge have, to some extent, changed the role of the foreign language teacher. Now that students may be researching a range of subjects which the teacher cannot know in detail, the teacher's role as facilitator and counsellor comes to the fore, directing students to sources of information and using advisory skills to elicit the best work from them.

Assessment techniques

As regards assessment techniques over the period under review, a major shift has been from negative to positive mark-schemes. Candidates are now rewarded for what they know, understand and can do and are not penalised for what they cannot do. Accuracy still features in all mark-schemes, both for written and oral examinations, but is now seen as only one aspect of assessment. Such features as fluency, range and variety are now assessed in productive writing and, as has already been indicated, other skills are given parity with writing. The effect is to spread the range of demands made on candidates more fairly, allowing them to demonstrate their strengths and to improve their marks overall. These moves towards a more equable distribution of marks are further strengthened by the steadily increasing detail contained in the mark-schemes and grids provided by all Boards. As far as students and teachers are concerned, there is now much greater certainty as to exactly how the marks are awarded, and how a student may concentrate on developing strengths to maximise the marks gained. As far as examiners are concerned, the advantage of the more detailed mark-schemes is that the element of subjectivity is reduced when making assessments. The grids also encourage examiners to award the full range of marks, rather than bunching marks around the centre point.

One further point should be made about changes in assessment techniques over the period reviewed, *viz* the increasing use of the target language in exam questions and student responses. The 'traditional' syllabus required just two pieces of written work in the foreign language – an essay and a translation from English. All literary questions, and of course the prose translation, were written in English. Compare that with the new criteria where no more than 10% of marks may be given for answers in English.

key points

- Examination components have changed, making direct comparisons over time difficult. The current examinations are different but may be considered equally demanding. Candidates are expected to cope with a greater range of tasks, to integrate their skills and to have an awareness of the cultural context and contemporary issues.
- Teachers have become more aware of the criteria by which examinations are assessed and are able to target their teaching more specifically to skills and criteria.
- The move towards teacher-marked options has changed the role of the teacher and students. Coursework is more student centred, inviting the student to become a researcher and allowing a personal choice of theme. The teacher's role is less directive and more consultative. Coursework has led to increasing involvement of Centres in the process of assessment. Students themselves are able to discuss and appreciate the assessment criteria applied by the teacher.
- Views about assessment have changed, leading to parity of skills, positive marking, greater use of the target language and greater objectivity in applying mark-schemes.
- The greater variety of assessment criteria is more concerned with a range of usable skills than with the limited requirements of accuracy in formal written tasks.

The path to AS and A2

Aims

This chapter aims to focus on the developments leading directly to the Dearing Report of 1996, and the new pattern of AS/A2 examinations.

The pros and cons of Exam Board diversity

A variety of approaches to A level assessment was followed by the different Boards, once the traditional consensus up to and including the 70s had been broken. The dangers of such variety are evident. In particular, since it was difficult to establish comparability across certain styles of test, it cannot be stated with absolute certainty that grades awarded by different Boards were exactly equivalent. The concern raised by such possible fluctuations explains the move towards increasing centralisation of criteria and control of syllabus definition evident in the most recent changes. However, before accepting the inevitability of rationalisation from the centre and the increased fairness it appears to bring, one should just point also to the strengths of the system we are now losing.

The Boards represented not just alternative approaches to assessment, but alternative cultures, where one Board might more appropriately meet the needs of a given centre than another, for example:

- In the 60s, the AEB launched, for the first time, alternatives to literary questions which demanded a wider knowledge of contemporary culture, and which were better suited to the interests of some candidates.

- The NEAB launched the idea of a dissertation as an alternative to literary examinations in its 1977 syllabus.

■ UODLE in the 80s introduced target-language examinations and the use of dictionaries met with a positive response from schools.

There are many benefits in examinations conducted according to a centrally prescribed set of criteria, but centralisation and rationalisation also limit the scope of individual experimentation and the range of choice.

Increasing standardisation

Since the 70s a series of steps have increasingly tended to standardise patterns of assessment.

■ **1982–87:** The Inter-Board Common Core was introduced according to a phased programme. The Common Core is important in marking the first step towards the common criteria which are now an accepted part of the examination system. It also marks the point at which the spread of assessment over all the language skills became standard practice, and at which Reading and Listening Comprehension became part of the battery of tests used by all Boards.

■ **1988:** The then government set up two separate agencies, the National Curriculum Council (NCC) for curriculum matters and the Schools Examination and Assessment Council (SEAC) for examinations. The progress of these bodies charts the increasing interventionism of central government in the examination process, which had previously been the province of the Examination Boards.

In 1993, SEAC formed a Modern Languages working party to consider, not only the changes at A level, but also developments brought about by the GCSE examinations first introduced in 1988, the National Curriculum proposals for foreign languages and the evidence of developments in good classroom practice. Also part of the discussion was the Advanced Supplementary examination (AS), introduced by Sir Keith Joseph when he was Secretary of State for Education. The AS represented the same level of achievement as a full A level, but fewer papers were offered as the course was supposed to occupy only half the teaching and examining time. The Boards had always had problems with AS in foreign languages, because of the inherent difficulty in deciding how to split a language syllabus in half. The 1993 working party proposed a new version of the Common Core. This should be defined for 50% of the A level examination and this defined 50% should therefore be identical with the AS (Advanced Supplementary) syllabus. These proposals formed the basis for the new syllabuses introduced in 1997 and 1998. The statements in the Common Core document show the way that views on A level language teaching were developing during the 90s:

> *Students should be made aware of the different ways in which concepts are perceived and expressed in the target language, particularly the concepts related to structure and cultural understanding. For this purpose their skills in listening, speaking, reading and writing should be developed by means of authentic materials, from a variety of written and spoken sources in the target language, upon which they should be prepared to perform a graded sequence of tasks, from directed through semi-directed to independent expression. These integrated skill tasks should allow students to demonstrate their competence in understanding for both general sense and specific detail, to manipulate the target language with confidence and to extend their powers of personal expression.*

Certain key features of the new philosophy stand out here: authentic materials; tasks in a graded sequence; integrated skills; an ability to manipulate the language allied to personal expression.

- **1993:** A merger of NCC and SEC (Schools Examinations Council, the successor to SEAC) produced the Schools Curriculum and Assessment Authority (SCAA).

- **1997:** A further merger took place, between SCAA and the National Council for Vocational Qualifications (NCVQ), the body responsible for overseeing vocational qualifications, to form the Qualifications and Curriculum Authority (QCA). The Education Act 1997 gave QCA a remit 'to promote quality and coherence in education and training.' QCA is a powerful force within education, having, as is stated on its website, 'a unique overview of curriculum, assessment and qualifications across the whole of education and training, from pre-school to higher vocational levels.'

A major step to current changes – the Dearing Report

The pace of change was certainly hotting up! The new syllabuses were not even in place when Sir Ron Dearing's *Review of qualifications for 16–19 year olds* was published in 1996, making proposals which would eventually lead to the new AS/A2 pattern for which teaching began at the start of the new school year in September 2000. The instructions for the Subject Core Development Groups set up by SCAA in 1996 were as follows:

Instructions for the revision of subject cores

The Development Groups are asked to decide what constitutes an appropriate AS and AL subject core in order to:

- *maintain the rigour of AL in the subject;*
- *provide a suitable basis for the development of AL and reformulated AS syllabuses;*
- *make provision, where appropriate, for the inclusion of Key Skills in syllabuses;*
- *make provision, where appropriate, for the inclusion of spiritual and moral aspects;*
- *make required learning outcomes more explicit at AS and AL.*

Of course, the most significant change proposed by Dearing, and subsequently incorporated into new syllabuses, was the introduction of a two-tier examination for A level. A new AS (now standing for Advanced Subsidiary), was to offer an examination at a level intermediate between GCSE and A level. Although a variety of patterns are possible, this effectively means an examination at the end of the first year of the sixth form.

Eventually, the debate on Dearing led to a new set of criteria, which, with various subsequent amendments, formed the basis for work on new syllabuses which started in early 1997. The work was shelved while the incoming Labour government reconsidered policy, and then restarted in late 1998. The timetable was tight. Boards (now reduced in number by a series of mergers) had to submit their proposals by April 1999. These proposals were then examined by QCA, which suggested (or demanded) changes to meet the criteria. Final approval was given by the autumn of 1999, so that Boards could run INSET for teachers and have the new syllabuses (now termed 'specifications') in the schools by early 2000, for first teaching in September 2000. Following this timetable, the first of the new AS examinations would be taken by students in January or June 2001, followed by the first of the A2 examinations in 2002.

key points

- The mandatory nature of the QCA criteria which provide the framework for the new AS/A2 exams is a product of a gradual increase in central control over the examination system.
- Although current thinking is that national examinations should be more standardised and rationalised, the diversity between Boards has, in the past, allowed for a certain amount of experiment and innovation.
- Since the 70s, a series of steps has increasingly tended to standardise patterns of assessment. The most decisive influence in recent years has been the Dearing Report, which is the basis for the new pattern of AS/A2 specifications.
- The other key development is the establishment of QCA, with a powerful remit for scrutinising Board procedures and papers and for carrying forward developments in the examination system.

3

The new pattern of AS/A2 examinations

The shape of the new criteria

The Boards developed the new syllabuses under the strictest criteria yet seen. The result, inevitably, is a significant coming together of syllabus specifications. Although each Board has attempted to maintain an element of individuality and difference, the criteria do set out to define 100% of the examination content and lay down specific allocation of marks under each of the assessment objectives. The rules and principles for development prescribed by QCA were as follows (with comments included in brackets):

- There should be a restriction on the number of specifications offered by each Board for a given subject. (In the past Boards had been able to develop alternative syllabuses, such as the London B syllabus for French, or the French with Business Studies of Oxford and Cambridge.)

- A level standard should be maintained. (Although it might be thought that this is something of a contradiction in terms, since 50% of the examination is specifically offered at a lower level.)

- A level should be composed of six examination units, divided equally between three units at AS and three at A2. (The six-unit model applied to almost all subjects with no chance for Modern Languages to argue that the subject might prefer more components to cater for specialities such as the oral examination, or to separate out different skills.)

- The units should be approximately evenly weighted, within the range 15–20%.

- AS and A2 should be equally weighted at 50% of the total assessment. (It is also the case that AS carries half the points of a full A level for purposes of UCAS weightings.) AS should be seen as a freestanding examination, available to students who might wish to gain a qualification at that level before concentrating on a smaller number of main subjects for A2. The A2 examination is not freestanding and can only be taken to combine with AS and form a full A level.

- Assessment sessions should be offered twice a year, in January and June. The AS examination can be taken as a terminal test at the end of one school year, or it can be taken in a modular fashion by Boards offering separate modules in the January and June sessions. Where centres or students wish to take both AS and A2 at the same session, they may do so, leaving AS assessment, if so required, until the end of the sixth-form course. The modular rules state that a unit (module) taken separately may only be retaken once and that the better result should then stand.

- A2 may also be offered as a terminal examination, or on a modular basis. (It should, however, be noted that modular entry for A2 in Modern Languages is unlikely, because of the rule relating to synoptic assessment. There has been concern in certain subjects that dividing a programme of study into separately assessed modules could lead to a lack of any overview of the subject. To ensure that students have such an overview, the synoptic element in the assessment programme specifies that 20% of A2 assessment must test the whole syllabus and understanding of connections between different elements of the subject. All modern language testing is synoptic in the sense that a range of skills is involved. To meet the synoptic requirement, Boards have had to designate the A2 modules which, taken together, cover all the modern language skills. If one takes the OCR specification as typical, two of the three examination units are so specified (Unit 4: Reading and Speaking; Unit 5: Reading, Writing and Listening). Since the remaining module is either Coursework (which is presented before the terminal examination) or Literature/Topics (which few, if any, students would be ready to take in January of their final year), the fact is that modular entry is not a realistic option for A2 Modern Languages.)

- Teacher-assessed coursework must not account for more than 20% of the total assessment in either AS or A2 and may not exceed 30% in the total A level assessment.

- Key Skills opportunities must be signposted. (In fact, Key Skills signposting presents something of a problem to syllabus developers in Modern Languages. Two of the Key Skills are not required by the Modern Languages criteria, *viz* Problem Solving and Application of Number. Of the remaining four skills, Communication, clearly the primary skill in this subject, is specifically excluded on the grounds that Communication as a Key Skill refers only to the mother tongue. At a time when one may expect student choice at A level to be influenced by the possibility of gaining Key Skills qualifications, this is bad news for language teachers. Hope rests with the Nuffield Languages Inquiry, whose report *Languages: The next generation,* published in May 2000, stated that the UK has no coherent approach to languages. One of the main proposals was worded as follows:

> **Designate languages a Key Skill**
> *Languages, by virtue of their direct contribution to economic competitiveness, intercultural tolerance and social cohesion, should have the status of a Key Skill, alongside literacy, numeracy and IT.*

Apart from the contested area of Communication, the Key Skill of Information Technology allows for some assessments to be carried out in Modern Languages. Clearly, there is no problem in meeting demands for the two remaining skills, Improving own Language and Performance and Working with Others.)

The criteria laid down other significant requirements, such as the proportion of English answers that could be allowed in the examinations (not more than 10% at each level). Dictionaries are to be excluded altogether from the exam room, including the preparation room for the oral test. Also excluded are other supporting materials such as literary texts, which had in recent years been allowed in 'open book' examinations.

The assessment objectives

When assessment objectives were introduced in the 1980s, they could vary in wording depending on the chosen emphasis of the Board. Very often, the four language skills which formed the basis of GCSE assessment objectives of 1988 were carried forward to A level, with the additional objective of cultural knowledge added at the higher level. A growing sense of dissatisfaction with the separation of the skills led to formulations that stressed the interaction of the skills and the possibility of mixed skill tests, e.g. 'Listening and responding'. The new assessment objectives built on this development to some extent. They are characterised, firstly, by the fact that they are common to all Boards and that their weighting is strictly prescribed as shown overleaf:

Assessment objectives

Candidates should be able to:

AO1 understand and respond, in speech and in writing, to spoken language;
AO2 understand and respond, in speech and writing, to written language;
AO3 show knowledge of and apply accurately the grammar and syntax prescribed in the specification;
AO4 demonstrate knowledge and understanding of aspects of the chosen society.

The assessment objectives are weighted as follows:

	AS	A2	A level overall
AO1	30%	25%	27.5%
AO2	35%	25%	30%
AO3	25%	25%	25%
AO4	10%	25%	17.5%

It is clear that this precise weighting and wording lays very specific demands upon syllabus writers and the way in which they fulfil the objectives while meeting other demands, such as the limitation on the use of English. The wording of AO2, for example, requires a task which tests response in speech to written language. That means that an oral examination must allow for some response to a written stimulus. The allocation of significant weighting to AO4 creates no problems at A2, where a literature or topics paper can test such knowledge. But it may be more problematic at AS, where chances for demonstrating knowledge of the culture may be more limited, for example forming part of a topic presentation in the oral.

The wording of AO3 came as something of a surprise when first encountered and clearly represents an attempt to meet criticisms of the way in which A level in Modern Languages is perceived to have gone 'soft' on grammatical accuracy. It is worth pointing out that the rather draconian phrasing of this assessment objective seems to have been softened in the actual mark-schemes produced by the Boards. Instead of being so wholly and exclusively concentrated on grammar and syntax, the AO has been taken to mean 'quality of language' in a more general sense and includes such criteria as range, variety and style.

Lists of grammatical structures

The wording of A03 refers to 'the grammar and syntax prescribed in the specification'. For the first time, the new specifications contain, for each language, a list of grammatical structures required at AS and A2. These lists have worried teachers, who have asked how they can hope to cover all the items in the AS list within the limited time to prepare for the examination. In fact, their worries are unfounded, in that the lists do little more than provide a sequence of headings such as might be found in any grammar book, and there is no requirement that Boards should test every item in the list on any regular basis. So, despite all the debate that went into the inclusion of these lists and the discussion about their status, it is doubtful, in the final analysis, if they have any significance at all. Supporters of a defined language syllabus at A level might have hoped for something more extensive and subtler in its explanations and more specific in its application to the tests set in the examination.

Unresolved issues – topic definition and levels of difficulty

Subsequent chapters will look more closely at the differing Board responses and at some of the general issues of language assessment raised by these criteria. There are just two points to make to conclude this chapter. Firstly, the one area not closely defined in the criteria is that of subject content in terms of topics or themes. So despite the close definitions and limitations as drawn up, this is an area where Boards do show some differences in approach. Secondly, one might well ask if there is any clarity over what exactly is the appropriate level of difficulty for AS language texts and tasks. Teachers know, of course, what their pupils can cope with after one year in the sixth form. But do all paper setters share exactly that same knowledge? There is, in fact, no generally accepted definition of difficulty nor criteria for drawing up a hierarchy of text-types and their level of difficulty. Difficulty may be lexical, structural or conceptual. One wonders by what criteria the QCA reviewers were able to satisfy themselves that all Boards were proposing text materials that were closely in line with the new AS standard, since the research doesn't exist which has established such criteria. The same is true for difficulty of test-types, for the balance between factual and inferential questions, and a number of other significant issues which will be pursued in Chapters 4 and 5.

key points

- QCA supervised the application of the new criteria by the Boards and reviewed their proposals for new specifications.
- Dearing's proposal that all subject studies should include aspects of study of the six Key Skills currently creates difficulty for language teaching, since the Key Skill of Communication applies only to the mother tongue.
- The wording of the assessment objectives for the new specifications suggests an approach which lays stress on mixed-skill approaches and renews an emphasis on grammatical accuracy in using the language.
- Although the framework of QCA criteria is tightly drawn, there is latitude in the area of topics which form the content of specifications and no agreed definitions of levels of difficulty of texts and tasks.

Key issues for debate

Aims

When syllabus specifications are finalised, decisions have to be taken, even if certain issues may not be fully resolved. It is inevitable that such specifications establish the pattern of assessment for a number of years. However, it is clear from developments already discussed in earlier chapters that the debate does not stand still. This chapter aims to raise a number of significant issues where the argument is ongoing.

In the developments outlined in the previous chapters, a number of key terms have appeared frequently and often shaped the discussions; such terms as 'topics', 'authenticity', 'target-language testing' and 'backwash effect'. Such usage soon comes to be established and even unquestioned. The use of 'authentic', for example, is so widespread that its meaning is rarely challenged. And who would think to question that 'topics' should provide the shape of syllabus content? Other issues have also been raised, such as the role of correct grammatical usage and the inclusion of a defined language content in the new specifications. Perhaps the most significant issue of all is the question of the appropriate level of language to be tested one year after GCSE in the new AS examination. This chapter offers a discussion of widely used terminology. It aims to open up issues for debate as a prelude to the following chapter, which offers a comparison of the responses by examination boards to the new criteria and an analysis of the implications of certain test-types.

Bridging the (grammar) gap

The term 'bridging the gap' has become something of a cliché for describing the progression from GCSE to A level. The achievements of GCSE students cover the range of skills and not all students will be equally proficient in all skills. In particular, the relatively limited number of marks given at GCSE for formal accuracy in the written language means that a student may gain a high grade while lacking a developed knowledge of the grammar content of the GCSE structure lists.

The place of formal instruction in grammar within the overall framework of a communicative methodology is a matter of constant debate. Also debated is the proportion of marks that should be allocated to grammatical accuracy in the examination. During the 90s, articles by university language tutors drew attention to a perceived drop in standards of formal correctness among first-year language undergraduates (Sheppard, 1993; McCulloch, 1995). These authors had no hesitation in blaming current teaching methods for the drop in standards and in seeing the examination boards as principally responsible. The critics claimed also that the lack of formal correctness was not balanced by any marked improvement in the communicative skills such as might be expected from current teaching methods. Such critics had a point, in that the aspect of language course and examination developments most open to criticism is the restricted view of communicative competence which sees fluency as the principle goal and structural accuracy and formal correctness as elements of limited importance. In the desire to escape from the tyranny of formal grammar-translation methods, there has been a flight to methods that are, in general, more motivating, more entertaining and more useful, but which leave significant gaps in the preparation of young linguists. As these linguists feed through the system into Higher Education, there are complaints about their knowledge and performance. Not only the level of written accuracy has been criticised but also aspects of fluency requiring some basic grammatical manipulations. McCulloch tells of university Germanists:

> ... *trying desperately to find solutions, above all, to the entrenched sloppiness and distaste for detail and accuracy brought about by five years of pre-university teaching geared to public examination structures that play down to a ludicrous degree the idea that accuracy and language awareness should be part and parcel at this stage of the language learning process.* (McCulloch, 1995)

It remains to be seen whether the conscious design of the QCA criteria to give formal grammar such a defined and prominent place in the assessment objectives will bear the desired fruit. I remain rather sceptical, as explained in Chapter 6 (p51) in the section entitled 'Teaching grammar: is there really any change?'.

Defined grammar lists

Defined grammar lists, as included in specifications for the first time, should provide a framework for teachers to plan their schemes of work. They were referred to earlier (p17) with the statement that the lists do little more than provide a sequence of headings. One might reasonably ask: what are they for? The inescapable logic of a defined list of structures should be that:

(a) there are structures which **must be tested** at a particular level;
(b) this defined language syllabus **will be sampled** in the examination.

The current lists satisfy neither of these criteria. The lists place no onus on Examination Boards to test certain items. In the French *baccalauréat* examination programme in foreign languages, to provide a point of comparison, the lists of grammatical features are much more detailed and specific. In addition, the examination contains a section called 'Linguistic Competence' which specifically tests grammatical knowledge. It seems that a chance to give specific linguistic content and progression to A level has been missed. The following debate about the place of such lists in a syllabus cannot change the current syllabus specifications, but it is worth airing the issue for future developments.

Clearly a defined content of grammatical structures for AS/A2 should start from the baseline of GCSE. But this immediately raises problems. The complete lists for GCSE include complex structures such as the conditional perfect in French, which are not likely to be part of the repertoire of any but the most able students. In an ideal world, a genuine progression through the National Curriculum to GCSE then on to AS and A2 would be planned as a unity. Since it seems that GCSE and A level planning can never take place in a unified way, any grammar lists for AS must necessarily repeat the full range of basic structures.

Whereas it can be assumed that the usual range of examination tasks will cover the general areas of agreements, conjugations, word order etc, it might reasonably be considered that an A level syllabus should be specific about testing certain key structures, receptively or productively, rather than leaving them to chance use in an essay or other short piece of writing. For example, receptively, the ability to recognise the force of a conditional sentence could be targeted by questions testing this awareness. Productively, the ability to use certain tenses might be **required.** If this train of thought were pursued, it would have a significant effect on test techniques by requiring tasks where structures could be specified. A decision would then have to be taken as to the coverage of such key structures in a single examination, or how often such structures should be sampled over a period of time. The key to such questions is whether there is any agreement about what an A level candidate **must** be able to do in the foreign language.

In proposing a defined-structure list of this kind, it is important to distinguish between the teaching programme and the testing programme. Because of the backwash effect (see below), the danger would be that the examination list would be seen as a maximum programme. But teachers dealing with texts in class are constantly meeting grammatical points that have not yet been covered. They then make a decision as to whether this is a point which should be treated in detail, whether it should be referred to, but with detailed treatment postponed, or whether it can be ignored at this point in the teaching programme. The existence of defined lists should not change this aspect of the teaching process.

So, a clear distinction must be made between the teaching process and the testing process and the examination is concerned with what should be **tested.** In this respect, there are three considerations when drawing up grammar lists:

(a) Exclusion: i.e. the structure does not appear in the list and will therefore not appear in the examination papers. (This might, for example, be the case with the French past historic at AS.)

(b) Inclusion receptive: i.e. the structure may appear in the examination tests but will only be tested for comprehension. Students must answer questions which require these structures to be understood, but they will not be tested on their own productive use of the structures.

(c) Inclusion productive: i.e. candidates may be expected to demonstrate the ability to use these structures productively.

To bring this part of the discussion to an end, the point may be made that our principal concern is to teach the foreign language. Topics or any other form of defined course content are of importance primarily as a vehicle for the language we are teaching. By failing to define more clearly the language content of our courses (this applies to the National Curriculum as much as to AS/A2) we have lost sight of our primary objective and been seduced by the breadth of subjects represented in topics and Areas of Experience.

Backwash effect

There is no real argument that examinations strongly influence teaching methods and programme content. It is doubtful whether there has ever been such pressure to shape the content of exams and the assessment methods and, as a result, to affect fundamentally the teacher's approach in the classroom.

For years, teachers complained that they could not find time for adequate oral practice in preparing students for the old O level examination. When GCSE was introduced in 1988 – an examination giving 25% of marks to speaking skills – teaching methods changed immediately to take account of these demands. The effect of the National Curriculum is also recognised:

> *The most important feature of the National Curriculum in Modern Foreign Languages has been the emphasis on increasing use of the target language in the classroom. The OFSTED report on the first year of implementation of KS3 notes that 'increased use of the target language by teachers led to improved standards'... (Modern Foreign Languages Key Stage 3, First Year, 1992–3, HMSO, 1993)*

In the same way, as indicated earlier, the AO3 requirement for correct manipulation of the target language in the new AS/A2 may well presage a return to a greater emphasis on formal grammar.

Topics as a framework for syllabus and teaching

The planning of A level modern language syllabuses around topics or, as at GCSE, 'Areas of Experience', has three clear advantages. It provides a pattern for organising information; it offers a principle for selecting materials; it provides a focus for treating the skills of language in an integrated and interrelated way. Once the traditional consensus had been broken and language that was predominantly formal and literary was no longer seen as the only register appropriate for examination tasks, another principle of selection was needed. How could the sheer range and variety of human life now available to examiners be contained within some manageable framework? Topics provided a solution. To nominate, for example, 'Crime and punishment' as an examination topic or a chapter in an A level coursebook provided a rationale for choosing texts, subjects for oral or written debate and a range of associated language.

Problems with a topic-based approach

There are three main problems with this approach. Firstly, topics lack clearly defined boundaries. Does the topic 'Holidays' exist in its own right, or as part of

'Tourism' or 'Leisure'? Secondly, there are numerous texts, especially literary texts, which are full of human and linguistic interest but which cannot be chosen by paper setters because they do not fall easily under any topic heading. Thirdly, the fact that a topic has been 'covered' in the coursebook and in the teaching programme does not necessarily mean that the candidate will be able to tackle with confidence any text on that subject encountered in the examination. Any topic has such a potential range of reference that the limited scope possible in school study could not conceivably prepare students for every eventuality in the examination. One has only to think of all the aspects of the popular topic 'Environment'. It covers every aspect of pollution (air, water, food, etc) and of conservation (plants, animals, countryside, etc). The only way in which there could be a direct link between teaching programme and examination task would be for a syllabus specification to lay down very specific guidelines for course and examination content. That would be undesirable for many reasons, and it is not surprising that topic content is the one area of the new specifications which has not been defined in any way by the QCA criteria. This is, therefore, where the Examination Boards show most variation, as the following lists illustrate. All Boards have made some effort to contain the range of topics for AS students and broaden that range at A2.

Topic range in Examination Board specifications

The following remarks may be made about the table opposite.

The inclusion of the rather vague 'Human-interest news items' in the OCR list is an attempt to include the possibility of texts which have a clear value in terms of interest and motivation for the students but which may not fit easily or obviously into one of the defined topic headings.

The lists shown provide a summary in each case and further details are given in the Board specifications. The range is, frankly, breathtaking. Under Education in the AQA French specification, for example, are listed Equal opportunities; Erasmus; Study abroad – exchanges; University systems and problems/issues, grants, funding; Agenda of change; *Collèges, lycées, universités, IUT et Grandes Écoles* – the main features; The *bac* option; *L'école laïque*.

What is clear from the lists is, first, the arbitrariness of topics chosen and what may be included under each heading. Secondly, the impossible range proposed. A single aspect of a single topic, such as *L'école laïque* referred to above requires a profound understanding, not just of French educational history, but of the whole

AQA	Edexcel	OCR

AS

Unit 1
Young people today
• Family and relationships
• Rights and responsibilities
• Leisure
• Healthy living
• Education
• Jobs and careers

Unit 2
Aspects of society
• Mass media
• Pollution, conservation, environment
• Immigration and multiculturalism
• Target-language country and Europe
• Target-language speaking world

Unit 3
• Based on topic areas listed for Units 1 and 2

GENERAL TOPIC AREAS

1 Day-to-day matters
• Food, diet, health
• Transport, travel and tourism
• Current affairs and media

2 Society
• Relationships, family, the generations, youth concerns
• Social issues, law, justice
• Leisure and the arts

3 The working world
• Education, training and employment
• Business and industry
• Information technology

TOPICS
• Media
• Advertising
• The arts
• Daily life
• Food and drink
• Sports and pastimes
• Travel, transport and holidays
• Human-interest news items

A2

Unit 4
Contemporary issues
• State and individual
• Distribution of wealth
• Health issues
• Transport issues
• Science and technology
• Racism
• Crime and punishment
• Future of Europe
• Global issues

Unit 5
The cultural and social landscape
• Set texts
• Literary topics
• Non-literary topics

Unit 6
Yesterday, today and tomorrow
• Based on topics listed under Units 4 and 5

GENERAL TOPIC AREAS

The three areas above plus:

4 The environment and citizenship
• Energy, pollution and the environment
• Politics and citizenship
• Campaigning organisations and charities

5 The international context
• Customs, traditions, beliefs, religions
• The European Union
• Worldwide problems

TOPICS
• Social issues
• The environment
• Education
• Law and order
• Politics
• Technological and scientific advances
• Human-interest news items

historical relationship between church and state. The fact is that the organisation of modern language syllabuses by topics has got out of hand. The drive away from irrelevance and the effort to establish inclusivity has resulted in unrealistic proposals and superficial treatment. Teachers are assumed, by such topic lists, to have an astonishing range of knowledge and reference. Students who may be struggling to come to terms with the difficulties of the language leap from GCSE to AS level are faced with a multiplicity of areas for study. At some stage it will be necessary for future syllabus specifications to step back from the proliferation of topic areas and establish an examination based on language skills with topics as a subsidiary element. But for the moment, the pattern is established.

Authenticity

The term authenticity is widely used and may be taken to refer either to text or task. A straightforward definition of authenticity of text might be that the text was originally written for a native speaker of the language and has not been edited in any way. This is a long way from earlier examination texts such as translations that were concocted especially for the examination. Many writers have drawn attention to the importance of authenticity. Bachman and Palmer (1996), for example, argue that it is 'a critical quality of language tests'. The current view of authenticity inevitably raises problems for the school student. It necessarily means that a given text may contain a wide variety of structures and lexis, and that such texts are difficult to set into a linear sequence of language learning. For this reason, coursebook writers and examination setters may back away from the pure version of authenticity and edit texts, even if only marginally, to exclude difficult items, or shorten the original. Then a second element of authenticity comes into play, the appearance and presentation of the text. So students are used to the idea that the text before them at least resembles an original newspaper article. Students are encouraged to drop the idea that they need to understand every word and phrase and learn how to develop reading skills which skim such an authentic (or 'authenticised') document for the information they need.

One might express some reservations about the meanings taken on by the word 'authentic'. At a more philosophical level, it may even be queried whether the experience of reading an apparently authentic article during a school period or a test can ever be truly authentic, in that the context of reading is wholly different from the original intention of the writer. Widdowson made this distinction as early as 1978, when he drew a distinct between 'genuineness' and 'authenticity'.

Genuineness is a characteristic of the passage itself and is an absolute quality. Authenticity is a characteristic of the relationship between the passage and the reader and has to do with appropriate response. (p80)

There is also a sense in which the debate about authenticity has so concentrated on newspaper and magazine articles and presentation, that one finds it necessary to argue if a literary text is to be reckoned as 'authentic'.

If authenticity of text is an ill-defined concept, authenticity of task is even more difficult to pin down. Carroll (1980) takes a hard line when he states:

A full application of the principle of authenticity would mean that all tasks undertaken should be real-life, interactive communicative operations and not the typical routine examination responses to the tester's 'stimuli'. (pp11–12)

This is just not an option available to a nationwide assessment system. In any case, the point has often been made that the testing situation requires a wider view of authenticity than the simulation of life-like tasks:

Real life is an impossible criterion for testing because a test is always to some extent a simulation. Harrison (1983, p91)

Davies (1978) refers to the pursuit of authenticity as 'chimerical'.

The effort to simulate real-life tasks led almost to an element of parody in the GCSE as it existed between 1988–1998. The effort, for example, to explain why the candidate has to leave a note for the mother of his penfriend after taking a phone call when alone in the house stretches credulity. All the task required was a short written statement in the foreign language. And is it all necessary? Lewkowicz (2000, p44) points out that, 'it is not known … how test takers perceive authenticity … It is also unclear whether the presence or absence of authenticity will affect test takers' performance'. There are no definitive answers in this discussion since there is so little hard evidence. We clearly have to accept a modified version of authenticity because of other pressures upon examinations. There remains just one key question: How do we best test the abilities whose development we want to encourage?

Target-language testing

Target-language testing was the subject of quite a heated debate in 1995–6, when proposals were brought forward to change GCSE in line with the recommendations for target-language teaching in the National Curriculum (see Neather *et al*, 1995). The 1988 model for GCSE established a testing model which made extensive use of English in all aspects of the examination. In Speaking (role-play scene-setting in English), Reading and Listening (questions and answers in English) and Writing (task setting in English), the tests set up a notion of transfer, interpreting or even 'hidden' translation as the basis for assessment. Changes came in 1998, but some A level syllabuses had already begun to move toward target-language testing (notably in the Oxford Delegacy syllabus of 1988). The movement was completed by the new criteria, applying to all Boards, which allow only 10% of marks to be awarded for questions in English.

Since the debates of 1995–6, the papers of the new GCSE and the specimen papers for the new AS/A2 examinations, teachers are familiar with the pattern and range of target-language tests. The pattern is established, but many questions remain unanswered. Chapter 5 will examine the tests proposed by the Boards in their specimen papers but some general remarks can be made here.

Measuring test difficulty

There is, first of all, the question of a hierarchy of difficulty for the various test-types. For example, true/false tests are generally considered to be an 'easy' option among test-types. In the QCA review of papers submitted by the boards in 2000, recommendations were made which clearly showed an attempt to meet such criticism. For example, Boards which had submitted true/false tests were told that such tests could not be considered valid and that the tests should be redesigned to include a third possibility, 'not in the text'. While it is certainly true that true/false tests give a 50% chance of a correct guess, this third option adds enormously to the difficulty. Scanning a text to see if an item of information is **not** present can be very time-consuming. Can we judge how much **more** difficult such a test is and how it compares for difficulty with other tests?

Another test type is related to true/false. A candidate is presented with a text and a range of statements, only a limited number of which matches up with statements in the text. Here again, the QCA review developed a rule (which appears to be quite arbitrary). If eight marks were awarded for this test, setters were told that the candidate should be faced with at least twice as many statements to choose from. The objective of such a range of distractors is clear; the test would possibly be too easy if the candidate had to choose eight from only twelve possibilities. But who is to say what the measure of increased difficulty may be by giving the candidate sixteen items to read instead of twelve? There is research to provide guidance here, but the detailed analysis of item difficulty seems to be concentrated in the area of testing EFL. No such analysis has informed the AS/A level debate.

Questions and answers in the foreign language

A further contentious issue is the use of questions and answers in the target language. Questions which rely on the candidate locating a piece of information in the text may expect a direct quote from the text as an answer. Does such an answer indicate merely the capacity to locate the answer or does it offer genuine comprehension? Boards have ways of phrasing tasks to meet this problem, e.g. OCR has the formulation (in the appropriate language): 'You should answer without copying extracts word for word from the text'. This suggests that the candidate's answer will be accepted if there is even a minimum manipulation of the material rather than simple regurgitation. The old Oxford Delegacy used to stipulate that an answer should not contain more than five words in sequence taken from the text. Another solution is to put questions which require candidates to draw inferences, to compare elements of the text, to evaluate the correctness of a piece of information. But such questions are of a higher order. In Chapter 6, a hierarchy of difficulty is suggested for the range of question-types.

Levels of text difficulty

With regard to defining levels of text difficulty at AS and A2 levels, there are no clear guidelines. Experienced teachers and examiners know in their bones what constitutes A level standard. Teachers know what their students can handle after one year in the sixth form. But this knowledge is nowhere described or categorised, which makes it problematic when devising a new examination such as AS. As we have seen, restricting the range of topics is not a way of limiting the difficulty of an examination; topics are just not linguistically defined. The grammar lists discussed above do not help to limit levels of difficulty at all. The bulk of grammar to be covered is contained within the AS lists, and with little refinement in terms of distinction between receptive and productive. Length of text is clearly a factor and all the Boards have indicated maximum lengths for examination texts; but we can all think of short texts which are linguistically very dense.

Reading texts

Difficulty in texts set to test Reading Comprehension (RC) may be lexical or syntactic or conceptual. Apparently transparent texts may carry a weight of meaning; you cannot get much easier, linguistically, than *'Je pense donc je suis'*, but would anyone claim that this is easy to understand? The same tripartite distinction of difficulty can be made with regard to texts for Listening Comprehension (LC), with the added dimension of reliance on the spoken word and a different style of text (see below).

A fruitful approach to defining levels of text difficulty would be to consider an analysis of text-types. As regards RC texts, the following possible approach is suggested by my colleague Ian Maun. (Private communication.)

> *It is apparent that not all text-types use the same grammatical points. Teachers and authors have long chosen weather forecasts and horoscopes as text-types which contain future tenses. Biographies and autobiographies are useful for examples of the past definite and the imperfect. Recipes, in French, use either the imperative or the infinitive.* **The grammar of a text is in part dependent on the function of that text.**
>
> *Here is an initial classification of text-types, each of which could be divided into sub-categories.*
>
> **Sequential:** *These are texts in which events follow each other in chronological or near-chronological order. There is little description, and few examples of subordination. The content is essentially concrete and indications of time may be frequent. The tenses will be those of narration, or the infinitive/imperative.*
>
> **Descriptive:** *In these texts, the narrative tenses (past definite, perfect) tend to be absent and the present and the imperfect predominate. Connectors will be of the co-ordinating type (*et, mais*). There will be subordination, particularly relative clauses. Vocabulary will be both concrete and abstract. Adjectives will play an important part in the text.*
>
> **Informative:** *Texts within this category explain, guide, offer advice, expound, summarise and forecast. They are categorised by affirmative statements, or more rarely, negative statements. The predominant tenses are the present and the future, although past tenses may be recruited to explain the historical roots of a situation. Vocabulary is more abstract than in the preceding categories. Subordination may be present and more logical connectors (*si, bien que, au cas où*) begin to appear.*

*Argumentative: The goal of such texts is to analyse, to persuade, to moralise and to prove. We could use the term **persuasive** for texts in which only one side of an argument is put, and reserve the term **argumentative** for texts in which two sides of a viewpoint are given. Texts of this type are the terrain par excellence of abstract vocabulary, of the logical connector and of subordination. In such texts, sentences will show balance and parallelisms of construction will be visible both within and across sentences.*

*Now, the way in which any of these texts is ordered is also, to a degree, dependent on the type of text that it is. Because of the very nature of language, all texts are, to some extent, sequential. There is, however, a distinguishing factor which divides our four text-types into two fundamental groups and that factor is **time**. We may distinguish between texts which are essentially **temporally** organised and those which are **textually** ordered. There is, of course, no absolute division that can be imposed, as some temporal texts have elements of textual organisation and some textually organised writings have temporal sequences within them.*

*The order in which the above text-types have been given corresponds to **a decreasing use of temporal organisation within the text and an increasing use of textual ordering**. Moreover, we may also see a gradation from the concrete to the abstract in terms of vocabulary and concepts.*

On examination, we will find that that temporally ordered texts are probably more simple, overall, than those textually ordered and that textually ordered texts involve more complex grammar. This is, of course, a broad generalisation, but it suggests a way in which students may be exposed to different types of text and different levels of grammar, namely by presenting temporal texts in the early stages of learning, gradually moving through texts with mixed temporal/textual elements and concluding with textually oriented types, thus creating a possible gradient of difficulty, both conceptually and grammatically. Since sequential texts tend to exhibit comparatively easy grammar (present, perfect, imperatives, etc) and relatively **concrete** vocabulary, it is logical to include them in teaching before the argumentative type, with its emphasis on the **abstract** and the **logical**. This would also fall in, one hopes, with the student's increasing level of intellectual maturity. Learners may thus move from the sequential to the textual, from the concrete to the abstract, and from the grammatically 'simple' to the grammatically more complex (grammatical simplicity, of course, being a relative and rather subjective notion). Such an analysis, allied to text length, may provide us with a basic framework for defining text difficulty more precisely and helping teachers and exam setters to hit the same marks.

Listening texts

As far as LC texts are concerned, we must first add the dimension of speech, as represented in conversations and dialogues. This is where the issue of authenticity again appears. Should text recordings be off-air, containing background noise and interruptions? Or should they be from 'authentic' sources, such as a radio broadcast, but re-recorded and edited for the examination? Certainly, authentic speech offers most difficulty as a listening task. Speech shows the following characteristics:

* repetition and reinforcement;
* padding;
* loss of thread;
* redundancy;
* change of direction;
* interaction.

In practice, spoken texts with these characteristics are not set in exams. Where two or more voices are present in a recording, this is usually in the more formal context of an interview.

Applying the above analysis to the range of spoken texts, we might suggest the following typology:

* **Descriptive**: e.g. *fait divers* or descriptive news item. The narrative has a temporal sequence, usually expressed in the past tense or the historic present.

* **Informative**: e.g. an announcement in a store, station, airport, etc. The content is factual, there is no redundancy and the reference to place, time and objects is specific. A further example of spoken informative texts would be radio and TV information such as is given in weather forecasts, traffic information, etc. Here there is recurrent vocabulary and a repetitive sequence.

  Informative texts may, however, go beyond the level of difficulty suggested by these examples, by making greater conceptual demands. Interviews are really informative texts with more variety of speakers. The information is obtained by an interviewer who puts questions to elicit the information from an expert.

* **Persuasive**: Such texts might have a single speaker with a message to put across.

■ **Argumentative**: Here, the two sides of an argument can actually be put by different speakers, possibly with the intervention of a third party as interviewer.

What is clear from any analysis of genuine listening materials is that, although they fall into parallel categories to reading texts in terms of this analysis, the discourse of spoken language, even in a formal presentation, is different from written discourse. The discourse is less dense and provides more support for the listener relying solely on the listening skill. This is why some of the most difficult listening texts are those where written texts are recorded and set as test items.

At some future date it will be necessary to face up to this issue of defining text difficulty. At the moment, judgements of text and task difficulty may be well founded in experience, but remain largely subjective. We shall see in the next chapter how Boards have responded to these problems in drawing up their specimen papers.

key points

This chapter has raised a number of issues for debate where answers are not clear cut. The purpose is to give teachers the information necessary to keep abreast of the debate. These issues are as follows:

- bridging the (grammar) gap;
- defined grammar lists;
- backwash effect;
- topics as a framework for syllabus and teaching;
- authenticity;
- target-language testing;
- measuring test difficulty;
- questions and answers in the foreign language;
- levels of text difficulty.

Overview of new examination tasks and test-types

How have the three largest Examination Boards responded to the demands of the QCA criteria? How do the new specifications face up to the issues debated in Chapter 4? It has already been pointed out that topic areas were not defined by the QCA criteria, and the differing responses of the Boards were given in the previous chapter. The allocation of marks for the skills is strictly prescribed by the weighting of assessment objectives set out in Chapter 3. This chapter does not, therefore, discuss how marks are awarded, nor how the Boards have allocated the tests between papers. The major factors to compare and consider here are the tasks proposed for the different skills and factors such as the length and difficulty of texts. The sequence followed is to present an outline of the proposed tasks for each skill and then a discussion of key issues. For the sake of simplicity, where examples are given or texts analysed, these are taken only from specimen papers for French. A dimension omitted from this limited survey is that represented by the mark-schemes. It is clear that to arrive at a clear idea of the level of difficulty represented by a given test item, one would need to balance the three elements; text difficulty, task difficulty and scoring procedures (mark-scheme). Such a detailed analysis is beyond the scope of this work.

The following analysis considers firstly the receptive skills of Listening and Reading at AS and A2. A consideration of the productive skills of Speaking and Writing then follows. In surveying the skills in this way, it should be borne in mind that the assessment objectives are framed to promote mixed-skill tasks even if mark-schemes must seek to give credit for separate competences.

Listening tasks at AS level

From the range of tasks available to test the listening skill, the Boards have chosen as shown in the following table.

|---|---|---|---|
1	(46 seconds) **Text-type** News item (information for radio programme): conceptually more demanding than straightforward descriptive news item **Task-type** Gap-fill multiple choice	(30 seconds) **Text-type** News item: descriptive; concrete lexis **Task-type** True/false/not in text	(42 seconds) **Text-type** News item: descriptive; concrete lexis **Task-type** Multiple-choice (three options)
2	(55 seconds) **Text-type** Announcement: future tense; extended sentence structure **Task-type** Question/answer in French	(1 minute) **Text-type** News item: descriptive; sequential; temporal organisation; concrete **Task-types** 1 Short answers giving information and figures if necessary 2 Find synonyms	(30 seconds) **Text-type** Radio advertising item: scripted publicity dialogue; persuasive; concrete lexis **Task-type** Gap-filling (words chosen from list including distractors)
3	(62 seconds) **Text-type** Information (two speakers but not dialogue) **Task-type** Guided summary in English	(1 min 30 secs) **Text-type** Interview: conversation/ informative; concrete lexis **Task-types** 1 Question/answer in FL 2 Write a total of 60–80 words in response to two questions of a more general nature, drawing on cultural knowledge	(1 minute) **Text-type** Answerphone recording: information; conversational tone; concrete lexis **Task-type** Guided production (short notes entered in table)
4	(3 minutes 45 seconds) **Text-type** Informative: radio interviews; four voices making separate statements **Task-type** Question/answer in French: last question is grammar cloze for inserting correct form of verb	(1 min 10 secs) **Text-type** News item: informative; concrete with some abstraction **Task-type** Guided summary (60 words) in English	

Total playing time of recorded material in specimen papers: AQA = 6 minutes, 28 seconds; Edexcel = 3 minutes; OCR = 2 minutes, 12 seconds (350 words).

Listening tasks at A2 level

From the range of tasks available to test the listening skill, the Boards have chosen as shown in the following table. Total playing time of recorded material in specimen papers: AQA= 7 minutes, 25 seconds; Edexcel = 3 minutes. 30 seconds; OCR = 3 minutes, 40 seconds.

Perhaps the most immediately striking fact about the listening tests is the variation in time of recorded material between the Boards. It is also clear, at both AS and A2 levels, that the stress is predominantly on informative texts. There is only one example (Edexcel AS passage 3, *Interview avec un lycéen*), of a text which has the tone of a genuine conversational interchange. OCR has an element of text variety with a radio advertising item at AS. Both OCR texts at A2 take the form of an interview, though they contain a good deal of factual information. Several of the informative texts look and sound very dense, e.g. Edexcel AS passage 4, *La croissance économique et la confiance des Français*. AQA has, at AS, a text with five speakers, but the voices are heard separately as part of a radio report and do not interact in dialogue. The other AQA texts lean quite heavily towards rather dense informative material, particularly at A2. Here, passage 2 has two speakers and an element of colloquial *reportage*. The remaining texts, all monologue presentations, might well be set as quite demanding reading comprehension passages.

	AQA	Edexcel	OCR
1	(1 minute 12 seconds) **Text-type** News item: informative; present and future tenses **Task-type** Short notes	(2 minutes) **Text-type** News item: descriptive and informative; some discussion; present, perfect, pluperfect **Task-type** Question/answer in French	(1 minute 50 seconds) **Text-type** Interview: informative; conversational exchange; two speakers; concrete lexis **Task-type** Fourteen statements: tick eight correct
2	(1 minute 10 seconds) **Text-type** News item: informative; two speakers; second speaker colloquial; present, perfect, pluperfect, imperfect tenses **Task-type** Nine statements: choose four which are incorrect	(1 minute 30 seconds) **Text-type** Continuation of same passage: informative/descriptive; single speaker **Task-type** Guided summary in English	(1 minute 50 seconds) **Text-type** Interview: informative **Task-type** Question/answer in French
3	(1 minute) **Text-type** News item: informative **Task-type** Gap-fill requiring grammatical manipulation		(1 minute) **Text-type** Answerphone recording information: conversational tone; concrete lexis **Task-type** Guided production (short notes entered in table)
4	(1 minute 30 seconds) **Text-type** News item: informative **Task-type** Question/answer in French		
5	(2 minutes 10 seconds) **Text-type** News-item: informative; range of tenses/complex sentence structure **Task-type** Question/answer in French: last question is guided summary in continuous written French (length not specified)		

Reading tasks at AS level (specimen papers)

Total words in reading texts: AQA = c840 (in addition, AQA Unit 2 has an anthology of pre-released texts which can be prepared during the course and which lead to written work (see below, p44); OCR = c1000; Edexcel = c600.

Reading passage	AQA	Edexcel	OCR
1	(Unit 1) **Text-type** Informative: newspaper report; range of tenses (present, perfect, imperfect, pluperfect, future, conditional of reported speech, passive voice); 230 words **Task-type** Fifteen statements: tick seven correct	**Text-type** Descriptive: present tense; (one perfect tense); 68 words **Task-type** True/false/not in text	(Unit 2) **Text-type** Descriptive text: 'authentic' presentation; mainly present tense; 260 words **Task-type** Matching task: match statements to brands
2	(Unit 1) **Text-type** Informative: newspaper report; mainly present tense and imperfect, conditional; 180 words **Task-type** Question/answer in French	**Text-type** Conversation (four written statements); present tense; 138 words **Task-types** 1 Matching task (match names to opinions) 2 Find synonyms	(Unit 2) **Text-type** Business letter: mainly present tense in business style; 160 words **Task-type** Gist translation into English
3	(Unit 1) **Text-type** *Bande dessinée:* pictorial/informative; about 60 words **Task-type** Matching task	**Text-type** News item: descriptive narrative; present, perfect and pluperfect tenses; 164 words **Task-type** Question/answer in French	(Unit 3) **Text-type** Publicity/advert: descriptive; tense: present (but sentence structure complex); 130 words **Task-type** True/false/not in text

	AQA	**Edexcel**	**OCR**
4	**Text-type** Informative/persuasive: statements of six opinions; 370 words **Task-type** Question/answer in French	**Text-type** Public notice: rhetorical questions and imperatives; 153 words **Task-type:** Question/answer in English	(Unit 3) **Text-type** Authentic magazine text: descriptive narrative; present and past tense; 112 words + captions to pictures **Task-type** Find equivalents of expressions in text

5		**Text-type**
		Newspaper advert/police
		publicity; 68 words + 86
		words rubric and guidance
		for written task
		
		Task-type
		Reading passage serves as
		stimulus for guided
		composition
			Text-type
			News report: descriptive;
			past and present tenses;
			345 words
			
			Task-type
			1 Write letter giving
			  opinions on text
			2 Cloze exercise: fill gaps
			  based on reading of text

Reading tasks at A2 level (Specimen Papers)

See the table on p40.

Total words in A2 reading texts: AQA = c1279; OCR = c850; Edexcel = c210.

Here again, as with length of recorded material in listening tasks, the variations in length of reading texts are considerable. Of course, all the Boards specify a considerable programme of reading in their Topics and Texts papers. It does seem anomalous, however, that the only reading passage actually offered as a reading task in the Edexcel A2 exam should be a shortish informative piece of just over 200 words, whereas AQA requires over 1,200 words of reading. At both levels, informative-type texts predominate. Edexcel offers a variation at AS passage 2, where a conversation is reproduced as four written statements. The OCR AS exam has texts set within a business/office context.

Reading passage	**AQA**	**Edexcel**	**OCR**
1	(Unit 4) **Text-type** Informative: newspaper report; present and future tenses; 70 words **Task-type** True/false/not in text	(Unit 6b) **Text-type** Informative: present, future and conditional tenses; 210 words **Task-types** 1 Question/answer in French 2 Translation English into French: 75 words based on original text	(Unit 4) **Text-type** Informative: 250 words **Task-type** Basis for oral discussion
2	(Unit 4) **Text-type** Informative: results of survey: 87 words of continuous prose in questions +160 words in response items = 247 words **Task-type** Find percentages: requires matching of statements to survey responses		(Unit 5) **Text-type** Informative/opinions: range of tenses; 630 words **Task-types** 1 Match statements to opinions of people quoted in text 2 True/false/not in text 3 Match definitions to words in text 4 Question/answer in French
3	(Unit 4) **Text-type** Informative: statements of five opinions; 280 words **Task-type** Question/answer in French		
4	(Unit 4) **Text-type** Informative/descriptive: range of tenses; 682 words **Task-types** 1 Fill table (match statements to info in text) 2 Question/answer in French 3 Translate section into English 4 Translate English sentences into French		

Summary of Listening and Reading test-types in AS and A2 specimen papers (three Boards)

		Listening	*Reading*
AS	**Non verbal**	Multiple-choice Gap-fill (multiple-choice) Gap-fill (choose items from list) Gap-fill (grammatical items) True/false/not in text Find synonyms	Tick correct statements Gap-fill (grammatical items) True/false/not in text Matching tasks Find synonyms Find equivalent expressions
	Written answers in FL	Short answers Question/answers (more extended) Extended essay Guided production	Question/answer Extended essays
	Written answers in English	Guided summary	Gist translation

A2	**Non verbal**	Gap-fill (grammatical items)
		Choose 4 correct statements
		  out of 9
		Choose 8 correct statements
		  out of 14
			True/false/not in text
			Matching tasks
			True/false/not in text
			Matching
			Find words from definitions

	Written answers in FL	Short notes Question/answers (more extended)	Question/answer Translation into French Guided summary
	Written answers in English	Guided summary	Translation into English

The above summary of task- and test-types in Reading and Listening must be seen as a preliminary approach to a more detailed analysis of the interaction of text and task at AS and A2 levels. Some conclusions may be drawn about the predominance of certain text-types and this can be related to the comments made at the end of Chapter 4 about the relationship between text-type and levels of difficulty. It would require a further stage of analysis to consider the lexical, structural and conceptual difficulties of the reading and listening texts and to relate those findings to task difficulty and scoring procedures.

Speaking tasks at AS level

From the range of tasks available to test the speaking skill, the Boards have chosen as follows:

	AQA	Edexcel	OCR
1	Response to visual and written material presented on a card. The candidate has twenty minutes to prepare. Questions are given on the card 'to provide guidance on the type of questions the examiner will ask'. Candidates respond to questions and discuss issues	Prepared oral topic. Presentation and discussion based on research of an aspect of the target-language country	Role-play. Candidates have five minutes to study a stimulus passage of not more than 120 words of background information **in English** relating to the situation in which they are placed. Situations are of a kind requiring the candidate to give practical information and advice, for example to a foreign visitor
2	Presentation and discussion of a topic chosen by the candidate		Presentation and discussion of a topic prepared by the candidate
3	General conversation on topics studied during the course		

The fact that presentation and discussion of a chosen topic is a key test-type in all speaking tests is because of the requirement to test AO4 (knowledge of the society). Testing such knowledge is only possible if the examination contains tests where the candidate makes an initial choice of subject matter and is therefore able to prepare meaningfully and demonstrate knowledge.

As regards the other objectives, it is clear that AO3 is assessed in the correctness of the candidate's language. Also assessment of AO1 is clearly part of such an interchange. However, the assessment of AO2 is more problematic. The wording ('understand in speech and writing the written language') clearly requires some response to a written stimulus in the assessment of speaking. Edexcel have no such written stimulus, but could perhaps argue that written texts had formed part of the candidate's preparation. OCR has a written stimulus for the role-play, but, rather surprisingly, in English. AQA has the stimulus provided by cards. Role-plays in the speaking test seem to have gone out of fashion! The OCR example is the only such test at either level of the examination.

Speaking tasks at A2 level

	AQA	**Edexcel**	**OCR**
1	Reporting and discussion. The candidate has twenty minutes to prepare two short articles **in English.** Questions and discussion in French form the first task of the exam	**Either:** Oral discussion of issues. Students outline an issue and justify their opinions. Discussion with the examiner then follows. Examiner will also introduce two further issues **Or:** Interpreting task	Discussion of short written stimulus in French
2	General conversation on topics studied during the A2 course		General conversation covering three general subject areas

Edexcel introduces an Interpreting task as an option; otherwise the main tasks required at A2 are substantially variations on general conversation. Both AQA and OCR have met the AO2 requirement that candidates should 'understand in speech ... the written language', though it may not be entirely clear (as with OCR's AS role-play) how this objective is met by reading material in English. As with AS, it is not clear how Edexcel meets this requirement, since there is no reading element within the exam.

Writing tasks at AS level (continuous writing in the foreign language)

Tasks requiring written English are not included here.

Test-type	AQA	Edexcel	OCR
1	1 French answers in response to questions on Listening text 2 French answers in response to questions on Reading texts	1 French answers in response to questions on Listening text 2 French answers in response to questions on Reading text	Business letter in response to English stimulus providing structure. 100 words maximum
2	Two pieces of continuous prose of 150 and 250 words in response to essay-type questions based on information in the pre-release texts	Two pieces of continuous prose of 30–40 words in response to Listening text Guided composition. Stimulus text and structure to follow. 140–160 words	Letter to newspaper following extended stimulus passage. 100–150 words

Writing tasks at A2 level (continuous writing in the foreign language)

See table opposite (tasks requiring written English are not included here).

There is more uniformity between Boards in the type of writing exercise required. Following the QCA criteria, specifications must allow for transfer between English and the foreign language in both directions. Questions and answers in the foreign language are standard. This is a test-type which could also bear closer inspection, because of the different styles of question, whether factual or inferential. (See the discussion of a hierarchy of question types in Chapter 6). All specifications have examples of guided and free composition in the foreign language, and all require extended writing, either in Coursework or in an exam paper on Topics and Texts.

est-type	**AQA**	**Edexcel**	**OCR**
1	Units 4 & 5 1 French answers in response to questions on Listening text 2 French answers in response to questions on Reading texts	Units 5 & 6c 1 French answers in response to questions on Listening text 2 French answers in response to questions on Reading text	Units 4 & 5 1 French answers in response to questions on Listening text 2 French answers in response to questions on Reading text 3 French answers in response to questions on an English text stimulus
2	Translation into French of English phrases based on items in stimulus text	Translation into French of 75 words of English based on stimulus text	80-word summary in French of information presented in English text
3	Unit 5 Two essays in French on set texts, or topics or literary topics. Length not specified (**Or** Coursework: 2 pieces totally around 1,600 words)	Essay of up to 250 words chosen from a variety of options	Unit 6 Two essays in French on set texts, or topics or literary topics. Total 500–700 words. (**Or** Coursework: one long or two shorter pieces; total up to 1,400 words)
4		Unit 5 Two essays in French on set texts, or topics or literary topics. Total 500 words. (**Or** Coursework: two pieces total up to 1,500 words)	

This chapter has offered a preliminary survey of the Boards' reactions to QCA criteria, as indicated by the specimen papers published with the approved specifications in 2000. The survey has been mainly descriptive and has only indicated in outline questions that might be raised as to levels of difficulty, comparability and equality of demand. What the survey does establish is that there is a need for significant research to establish clear hierarchies of difficulty in fixing the appropriate level for AS and A2 examinations in Modern Foreign Languages.

key points

This chapter provides a detailed analysis of the content of AS and A2 examinations as proposed by the specimen papers of three main Boards:

- Perhaps the most immediately striking thing about the **listening** tests is the variation in time of the recorded material between the Boards. It is also clear, at both AS and A2 levels, that the stress is predominantly on informative texts.
- As with the length of recorded material in listening tasks, the variations in length of **reading** texts are considerable. At both levels, informative type texts predominate.
- In **speaking,** only OCR shows a desire to keep some form of role-play. Edexcel maintains the interpreting option which had already been established in the earlier A level syllabus. Otherwise, the pattern of general conversation and topic presentation are the common features of oral exams.
- There is more uniformity between Boards in the type of **writing** exercise required. All specifications have examples of guided and free composition in the foreign language and all require extended writing at A2 level, either in Coursework or in an exam paper on Topics and Texts.

Teaching for the new specifications

Schemes of work and teaching methods

New teaching programmes and schemes of work must be developed to meet the demands of the new specifications in foreign languages. This is clear from the novelty of the requirement to prepare students for the new AS exam in one year from GCSE. Even if some schools decide to enter students for AS and A2 together after a full two-year course, AS standards provide a waymark at the end of the first year. It is a fair assumption, however, that a majority of centres will enter candidates for AS after one year. Teachers are therefore faced with very limited time to reach a level that is still not clearly defined. There will be an obvious tendency to go beyond the perceived AS standard to ensure that students are not disadvantaged. This was pointed out by a headteacher in an article in the *Times Educational Supplement* of 18 May 2001.

> *Staff are not sure what standards the exams are going to be ... In their anxiety to make sure their students are going to do well they have taught to the standard that A level has typically been.*

Ideally, it will be necessary to use the time available after GCSE exams and before the end of the summer term, rather than leave the start of the AS course until September. The consolidation of GCSE knowledge, the work to extend vocabulary and handle more difficult concepts in AS texts, all these require careful planning and the need for the student to develop autonomy and personal learning strategies. (A great deal of help in this regard will be found in Barry Jones's Advanced Pathfinder 2: *Developing learning strategies,* CILT, 2001.)

New programmes and schemes of work therefore require detailed planning and more student autonomy, but they do not inevitably mean new teaching methods. Major changes in teaching methods have certainly been needed over the years of development described in Chapter 1. The growing importance of the listening and speaking skills; the shift from mainly literary texts to contemporary topics; the changes in exam tasks from translation and essay to a variety of mixed-skill tasks – all these developments have forced teachers to make radical changes to classroom practice. Patterns of good practice have been developed, and the immediate conclusions to draw from a study of the new criteria and the first examples of new exam papers is that these patterns remain valid. This is clear from the fact that publishers are able to re-issue successful coursebooks with few changes. The aims of this chapter are therefore:

- to discuss more general issues relating to skills, strategies and processes in language learning;

- to draw attention to aspects of the new specifications which might require special consideration, notably the stress on grammatical accuracy;

- to summarise successful approaches to sixth-form teaching as they have developed over the last few years and have been exemplified in a range of coursebooks.

Skills, strategies and processes

In talking about teaching and testing foreign languages, one usually goes straight into a discussion of skills development. But there is a level of discussion which should precede the debate about the practical skills. What are the fundamental processes that underlie skill getting and skill using? By what strategies do successful language learners develop their skills? This question is of key importance, given the limited time available for reaching AS level and the growing importance of student autonomy in the learning process. A valuable discussion of what is meant by strategies and process is given by Bialystok (1992). She suggests an initial pattern where language use is a product of both processes and strategies. She categorises processes as follows:

Process is generally used in psychology to refer to the mental steps taken to carry out a cognitive activity. Processes can be completely unconscious and inaccessible to the individual ... [or] are more amenable to inspection and modification. Mental processes of both these kinds control communication ... relatively unconscious processes are responsible for generating well-formed utterances according to the rules of grammar, while more conscious processes are involved in monitoring the conversation and determining the intentional content of utterances. (p15)

But a strategy requires more than a process. For example, carrying on a conversation would involve more active strategies of communication. Learning also involves a certain number of more or less unconscious processes and strategies which include the various techniques we adopt to help us to remember new material – for example, learning new vocabulary. Strategies may be limited in time, a reaction to an immediate situation to overcome a communication problem.

The pattern she suggests might be indicated as follows:

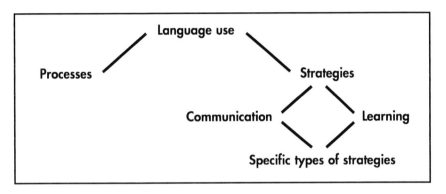

But repeating a strategy, for example, inference in reading, may allow it to become a process. Bialystok suggests that two components underlie language processing: the analysis of linguistic knowledge (not necessarily conscious) and the control of linguistic processing. Perhaps the idea of process as internalised strategy is more helpful to teachers than the rather discredited notion of habit formation, which seems to lack a mental or cognitive dimension. The debate about strategy is also useful because it brings together the twin ideas of communication strategies and learning strategies. Strategies may be more important than skills, in that long-term success in using skills and in applying skills may require the teaching of wider strategies of comprehending the unknown and communicating with limitations. Individual learning strategies are an important part of this approach. How can the student be made aware, for example, of his/her own strategies in learning and retaining new vocabulary in a foreign language? (See Barry Jones, *op cit,* for detailed practical advice on developing such strategies.) The mention of student awareness leads on to issues of language awareness and learner training.

Language awareness and learner training

The idea of language awareness is widely known as a result of Eric Hawkins's work (1984), although, sadly, the curriculum does not really allow for courses in language awareness as such. Raising consciousness about the workings of one's mother tongue might be seen as essential to an understanding of the way a foreign language works. Perhaps the otherwise laudable concentration on using the target language has led to a reduction in the chances to make explicit comparisons between L1 and the FL. Learner training is not so well known among teachers of foreign languages as language awareness, although the term is widely used in EFL. The idea of learner training is to help learners consider the factors that affect their learning and discover the learning strategies that suit them best. The emphasis is on **how** to learn rather than on **what** to learn. Learner training is based on the following two assumptions:

■ individuals learn in different ways and may use a variety of learning strategies at different times;

■ the more informed learners are about language and language learning, the more effective they will be at managing their own learning.

So learners need to be informed about the language (by language awareness activities), about language learning techniques (by experimentation and reflection) and about themselves as language learners (by self-assessment). Apart from their importance to individual language learners, this stress on self-awareness and learning how to learn takes up the themes of two of the Key Skills discussed earlier, Improving own Learning and Performance and Working with Others.

Steps in learner training

Learner training should be seen as wider in scope than study skills, which involve the learner in specific tasks and activities, e.g. dictionary use, note taking. Ellis and Sinclair, in their book *Learning to learn English* (1989) suggest skills training covering six skills, and within each skill, seven steps to develop learner autonomy:

Skills		Steps within each skill	
a	Extending vocabulary	a	How do you feel about ...?
b	Dealing with grammar	b	What do you know about ...?
c	Listening	c	How well are you doing?
d	Speaking	d	What do you need to do next?
e	Reading	e	How do you prefer to learn/ practise?
f	Writing	f	Do you need to build up your confidence?
		g	How do you organise ...?

Such an approach stresses the autonomy of the learning process. Students take more responsibility for their own learning. The approach would also fit closely with the aims of the Key Skills mentioned above. Of course, one of the implications of such an approach is that teachers might have to face some undesirable opinions. Would one be resistant to students who said they learned best when always given the English alongside the target language? Or who preferred to write words down before being asked to retain them? We all tend to get stuck into our current thinking and to reject individual preferences which may be quite justified. Current practice is strongly in favour of target language teaching, but we might need to consider an exploration of the relationship between the TL and L1, and decide how best to encourage those students who want to reflect on this relationship.

The greater involvement of students in taking responsibility for their own learning has already been developed in the Coursework options taken for A level. The new AS/A2 pattern requires significant further moves in that direction if teachers are not to be swamped by the pressures to teach for the new courses.

Teaching grammar: is there really any change?

Perhaps the most obvious new element of the AS/A2 specifications is the stress on grammatical accuracy. This emphasis is clear from the formulation of AO3 (see pp16–17) and the allocation of 25% of marks to that objective. It is also clear from the stipulation that productive language must always be assessed for accuracy.

Finally, there is the novelty, as far as English exam syllabuses are concerned, of a defined list of grammatical structures. (See the discussion on this topic in Chapter 4.) All this must be kept in perspective. It is a fallacy to assume that grammatical accuracy ever went away and is now being reclaimed as significant. Teachers of sixth-form students have always been fully aware of the need for correct grammar. But grammatical accuracy has ceased to be to the sole significant yardstick by which performance is measured, and positive marking allows even students with weak grammar to gain credit for their work. It is not obvious that the renewed focus on grammar suggested by the weighting of AO3 and the addition of the structure lists will necessarily make a difference to the teaching of grammar. The structure lists do not impose essential test items onto exam setters, so they can really only be regarded as advisory checklists, such as might be selected from any grammar index. The Board mark-schemes show no return to negative marking or the penalisation of error. The generalised mark-schemes for 'quality of language' are of the kind that have become commonplace in recent years. The only explicit grammar test which has been added to the repertoire by the new specifications is the OCR multiple-choice cloze set in AS Unit 3 (Reading & Writing). If we take the first actual AS example, set in January 2001 French, candidates first read as a stimulus text a passage entitled '*Pourquoi les femmes snobent-elles l'euro?*' to which they must respond with a piece of continuous prose of between 100 and 150 words. They are then faced with a series of sentences requiring a gap to be filled by a correct grammatical item, for example:

1 Les femmes ne sont pas   **a** séduit

                            b séduites   par la monnaie unique.

                            c séduire

2 Les femmes sont souvent obligées **a** à

                                     b de   faire les courses.

                                     c pour

This is a style of test which is not uncommon in TEFL and which has the virtue that it does put the student on the spot to come up with a correct form, in a way that more global descriptive criteria do not. For example, the Edexcel A2 translation from English into the foreign language is marked on a range of positive criteria, for which the sequence referring to Accuracy is as follows:

Mark 14–15	*Highly accurate ... effective manipulation of a wide range of structures.*
Mark 12–13	*Very accurate with only a few minor errors.*
Mark 10–11	*Mostly accurate, with errors of grammar and structure mostly minor.*
Mark 8–9	*Quite frequent minor and occasionally major errors.*
Mark 6–7	*Intrusive errors in grammar, structure and lexis.*
Mark 4–5	*Frequent major errors in grammar structure and lexis.*
Mark 1–3	*... few examples of correct grammar, structure and lexis.*

(Edexcel specification, p41)

Such a mark-scheme may have obvious virtues but it does not actually come down hard on specific error. Despite the apparent shift of emphasis introduced by the weighting of AO3, the evidence of such mark-schemes and tests where accuracy is assessed, is that changes could have gone further.

Even so, there is certainly a change of climate regarding grammar. Students are keen to have the support given by grammatical patterns and the most recent coursebooks give a clearer focus to grammar than has previously been the case. The notion that communicative fluency does not need the support of correct grammatical patterns was always a fallacy. Without reverting to the grammar-grind of the past, an element of formal grammar teaching is now seen as central to developing good language habits. So teachers can combine formal grammar teaching within their programmes and not feel a pang of guilt! One can recommend no more than that teachers continue to cover the grammatical ground methodically, to give exercises on specific grammatical points and attempt to refrain from tearing their hair out when their patient and repeated explanations are ignored or forgotten.

Teaching for skills development

It was pointed out earlier that the assessment objectives in the QCA criteria lead to a focus on mixed-skill tests. It has become commonplace to talk about testing the 'four skills' – Listening, Speaking, Reading and Writing – as if they were quite distinct. And yet, language skills in real life are rarely separate. We may want to speak in response to something we have heard, or write a reaction to something we have read. The idea that language skills are actually integrated lies behind current approaches to testing.

But although rather too extensive use of English in questions has led to some exaggerated examples of separate skills **testing,** the best **teaching** practice has always seen integrated skills as fundamental to teaching languages in the sixth form. Starting from the foreign language text, whether written or spoken, the best practice works from reading or listening comprehension through to spoken or written production. The sequence was effectively described in a significant article by Ralph Gaskell as long ago as 1977 and has been refined since then and used as a basis for the approach of numerous coursebooks.

One starts from the text, which may take a variety of forms: an article, a literary extract, a cartoon or video; a radio broadcast, tape/slide presentation, Internet item. A three-stage sequence is then followed:

> *The first step in the exploitation of texts is a process of discovery: of information, of language or of both. Next, in intensive work, the language must be sorted and practised and finally the pupil must be encouraged to use his acquisitions in many varieties of context.* (Gaskell, *op cit,* p27)

The table opposite sets out the sort of tasks which might form the basis of such an approach.

The first 'Discovery' stage might be preceded by the teacher introducing the theme, raising interest and curiosity to know more. In the case of a listening text, there may be a number of pre-listening tasks to develop listening skills (see below). But the discovery itself is carried out largely by the pupil working alone or with a partner. This is a stage of student autonomy, where students may set their own pace of learning, make use of reference materials on an individual basis and draw individual conclusions. The tasks are set and guided by the teacher or coursebook, but there is no need at this stage for systematic direction of the discovery process by the teacher. It is in the middle stage, 'Sorting and Practising', that the teacher is more directive. This is where the basis for correct use is laid by more formal tasks which systematise the grammar, draw on what is already known and shape the learning process. This is also where methods which some might consider 'old-fashioned' have a place in fixing the new knowledge. Short passages for translation or re-translation, dictation, learning by heart and formal grammatical practice such as inserting correct adjectival endings or practising the use of the relative pronoun, all these have a place at this stage in the learning process. Finally, in the third stage of 'Use' of the language, the student must be encouraged to apply the information 'discovered' and the formal elements 'sorted and practised' and become more independent and adventurous. This is where the productive skills or Speaking and Writing take precedence.

Stage 1	Discovering the text – collecting information and language	
	Anticipation	e.g. using headlines, pictures, layout, etc
	Scanning	e.g. locating specific information
	Gist reading	e.g. true/false tasks; gist questions
	Language analysis and collection	e.g. find words from definitions; find synonyms; find English equivalents
	Structure and sequencing	e.g. study relations within sentences; fill gaps

Stage 2	Working around the text – sorting and practising the language	
	Written consolidation	e.g. question and answer; sentence/phrase-building; translation and retranslation; dictation
	Grammar practice	e.g. grammatical manipulation and rephrasing; partial or total reconstruction of the text

Stage 3	Working away from the text – using the language independently	
	Summary	written or oral
	Comprehension questions	written or oral
	Composition writing	e.g. argue pros and cons of an issue raised in the text
	Oral presentation of topic	Student speaks for up to three minutes with written headings as an *aide-mémoire*. The presentation is then followed by discussion initiated by the teacher

Although this pattern may be appropriate, with variations, for either reading or listening texts. It is worth discussing, at this point, some differences in approach.

What exactly is reading comprehension?

This seems a rather obvious question to ask, but in fact, reading comprehension can operate at several levels. It might mean understanding individual words or it might extend to larger units such as short phrases, sentences and, finally, a grasp of the whole text. Exam papers have been developed over recent years so that tasks set out to test reading comprehension at each of these levels. There are tasks which focus on words and other exercises which test structures or comprehension of longer sequences.

To test comprehension of the more advanced reading skills, questions can be set which ask for comparison and evaluation of differing approaches to the theme. So the answer to the question, 'What is reading comprehension?' is linked to another question, 'How is reading comprehension tested?', and we might list quite a number of different activities which are involved in the process of testing reading comprehension in a foreign language. Some of those activities are listed below. Not all these activities are represented in every examination paper, but the categories given below indicate the thinking that lies behind the tasks that examiners may set, whether non-verbal or requiring more extended written answers. The following table also suggests a hierarchy of question setting that examiners may adopt. The sequence may also be of positive help to teachers setting their own tests and planning teaching sequences.

Activities involved in Reading Comprehension	**Locate** identify, recognise, select ... one or several elements of information already present in a text **Reorganise** classify, order ... diverse information explicitly present in a text **Compare** distinguish, associate ... information with a view to extracting similarities or differences present in one or several texts **Infer** deduce, predict, interpret, extrapolate ... the information contained explicitly or implicitly in the text **Appreciate** distinguish a fact from an opinion or a feeling ... evaluate the correctness of a piece of information; judge whether an action is good or bad

(Translated and adapted from Lussier, 1993)

The nature of listening comprehension

Listening comprehension may be needed for direct linguistic interaction, for example when taking part in a conversation. This aspect of listening forms part of the oral exam. When there is no such direct linguistic interchange, listening comprehension takes the form of **mental** interaction, for example, decoding and reacting to news items, reports, announcements, broadcast interviews or discussions. In real life, listening of this kind may have no actual linguistic **output,** unless we make notes on a radio programme or take down details of times and dates from a recorded message. In the exam, there has to be a language output for the purpose of assessment, hence the range of tasks on exam papers requiring a response which indicates recognition and understanding.

Listening comprehension requires us to decode information using phonological, lexical and grammatical clues. It is this complexity of response, allied to the fleeting nature of the spoken word, which makes examination tests of listening comprehension potentially stressful for candidates. In an age which is so geared towards the visual, close listening of the kind required for language exams is a skill that must be trained. Classroom approaches to listening skills often just make use of exam tasks as practice. But here also, there are strategies which can be trained and developed. Some ideas are given below ('Developing listening skills').

Some of the trauma caused by listening exams in the past has been removed by the change in delivery of this test. In the past, all candidates at a centre would gather in a classroom or larger hall to listen on a loudspeaker to the listening exam and would be restricted to hearing each passage twice. All Boards have now adopted the approach first pioneered by the Oxford Delegacy, where candidates are allowed individual control of their own tape in a so-called 'Walkman-style' examination. The Walkman style removes the pressure caused by knowing that if you failed to understand the passage in two hearings, you had no chance. However, the approach does bring its own problems, notably time-management and control of the tape. Part of the teacher's concern will be, not just to develop the skills and strategies for successful listening, but also to guide students to look at the exam tasks as a whole, note the allocation of marks, not get bogged down with one knotty problem and pace themselves through the whole paper. Getting lost on the tape is a potential problem for a student, but is largely removed if student cassette players have a rev-counter from which they can note their place and return to it if necessary.

Developing listening skills

The three-stage approach presented earlier is as valid for listening as for reading texts. However, there are also specific ways in which listening skills can be developed and encouraged. Learning to listen is a continuous process of the listener attempting to increase his/her capacity to interpret and respond to language events. In classroom approaches, controlling the level of difficulty is important to prevent students from being demoralised. Students should be encouraged to develop their capacity for interpreting a text by carrying out some of the following processes:

- Deduce the meaning of unfamiliar words.

- Infer information not explicitly stated.

- Recognise indicators for introducing an idea, changing topic, emphasis, clarification, expressing a contrary view.

- Construct the main idea or theme in a stretch of discourse and distinguish the main point from supporting details.

- Predict subsequent parts of the text.

- Identify elements in the text that can help to recognise a pattern of organisation.

The following is a short list of possible approaches to developing these listening skills.

Running memory exercise

This drill sets out to train the listener's short-term memory which must be trained to store information decoded in the foreign language. The student, listening individually, notes a word heard in a sequence, then stops the tape soon after. He or she then repeats the section of the tape from the word to the point where the tape stopped.

Listening ahead

The teacher stops the tape at a certain point and asks students to complete the rest of the sentence. Lexical, grammatical and semantic cues can help to suggest the continuation.

Following a written text

Listen to a text and read it at the same time. This has limited value for examination preparation, but is valid in helping to bridge the gap between reading perception and writing.

Make notes on a text

To focus the listening skills, a summary or notes are useful.

Transcription

This is a form of very intensive listening, similar to dictation, but with the opportunity of replaying the tape so as to train the ear to pick up details not at first heard.

Productive skills – Speaking and Writing

As far as preparation for the Speaking test at AS and A2 are concerned, nothing has changed. The tests in the examination are mainly topic presentation and general conversation. There is one example of a role-play (OCR AS) and the rather specialised demands of the Edexcel interpreting option. The three-stage pattern of progression presented earlier would generate more structured speaking practice in the second stage, practising new grammatical structures or new topic vocabulary. All current coursebooks suggest pairwork activities and other tasks for developing fluency and accuracy. Students are then guided towards the third stage where they can bring together their knowledge of the topic and the language 'discovered' earlier to develop presentations and expressions of a point of view. Specific help and advice on developing speaking skills are given in Anneli McLachlan's book *Advancing oral skills* (Advanced Pathfinder 1, CILT, 2001).

The process for writing is similar. The second stage gives the chance to practise new material in targeted tasks aiming to clarify the grammar and use new structures and vocabulary. This is also the place for writing answers to questions on a text, such as are set by all the Boards. In addition, this phase includes guided writing tasks, such as writing paragraphs focused on a particular issue, or putting together a piece of continuous prose from a set of notes provided by the teacher.

In the third stage, working away from the text, students will develop skills of continuous extended writing, as in a summary or an essay. At AS level, all the Boards require writing tasks of up to 150 words with varying degrees of guidance or stimulus provided. At A2, extended essays are required either in the Topics and Texts unit or in the Coursework option. For extended writing it is important to develop an approach to the writing **process.** In any piece of writing outside of an examination, an author knows his/her audience, the purpose of the task and the level of formality to adopt. It will also be normal to plan and draft a document before editing and redrafting a final version. This same process can be followed in the preparation for writing tasks in the foreign language. Skills can be developed in sequence, starting by making notes on a set topic, then planning sections and paragraphs, writing a first draft for discussion and finally editing, checking and rewriting as necessary.

In conclusion to this chapter on the teaching implications of the new examinations, it can be stressed again that there is a considerable measure of continuity as far as classroom methods and approaches are concerned. Teachers are not required to make the major changes in teaching methods required by earlier examination changes. The best practice developed over recent years of using authentic texts and interactive methods remains valid, but needs to be adapted to the changing demands of the examination tasks in the different skill areas. There are a variety of course materials on the market which specifically meet the demands of the new qualifications.

key points

- All language teachers know about skills development. But skills depend on personal strategies of active language use. How can teachers develop those strategies in their students?
- What strategies and processes, as well as skills, are involved in language learning?
- There is little in the new specifications which leads to major changes of direction in teaching methods. The examples of good practice developed over recent years are still valid, but need to be adapted to the specific demands of the new tests and exam tasks.
- A possible three-phase pattern of approach to a teaching sequence involving all the skills is explained. Teachers will find it helpful to follow this sequence from the point of introducing students to new material to the end product where the student has acquired the material and can make active use of it in the productive skills.

Teaching and assessment in the vocational sector

A publication concerned with post-16 examinations must necessarily consider the vocational sector as well as the traditional academic path to A levels. This is surely a significant fact. In the past, vocational and academic qualifications have occupied quite different worlds. In their development they had nothing in common. The demands of industry and commerce were seen as quite distinct from the demands of the university. But those worlds are no longer separate. Students in today's sixth forms expect to be able to follow courses and take qualifications across the whole range of their interests and with a variety of careers in view. Divisions between vocational and academic qualifications begin to look artificial. One major problem which has been tackled in recent years is the move to bring order and comparability into the often confusing variety of vocational qualifications. The fact that responsibility for all examinations, vocational and academic now rests with a single body, the QCA, means that a common framework of qualifications is being developed. There remain significant problems, one of which is to ensure that the two paths to qualification have not only a common, transparent framework, but also parity of esteem. The further integration of qualifications in both areas is certainly one of the most significant areas for development in the immediate future. This chapter aims to provide a survey of vocational qualifications post-16.

Background

There are a number of issues which provide the background to an understanding of the developing area of vocational qualifications. These may be summarised as follows:

- Curriculum 2000 provides a new qualification framework to facilitate diversification of learning. This flexible structure aims to encourage pupils to mix subjects.

- A boost to language teaching and learning was given by the Nuffield Languages Inquiry which asked whether knowing English was sufficient in a global market and proposed measures to promote language learning.

- Recent years have seen the globalisation of the business environment and competition for trade as well as growth of the service industries. In March 1999, the Department of Trade and Industry published a *Guide for exporters* as part of its National Languages for Export Campaign.

- Higher Education is not excluded from this picture. Universities are increasingly offering courses that appeal to non-specialist MFL learners in addition to core programmes, generally as business languages. Distance learning is growing and self-access centres for languages are expanding. Expansion of access to the Internet in countries not using English is widely publicised and the European white paper, *Teaching and learning towards the learning society* (HMSO, 1995) recommends that all European citizens should have three languages.

Types of work-based tasks and examples

Teaching vocational languages enables teachers to incorporate meaningful activities that are relevant to students' learning in other subjects. In particular, one might mention:

- Research and presentation activities (research on an area of tourist interest or product information, where the student presents results to the class). Such activities promote initiative, make use of authentic material (brochures, catalogues, reports, web-based resources) and enable learners to put into practice what has been learnt (making choices, making phone calls, sending faxes and e-mail, summarising, reporting, presenting).

- Pro-active and reactive tasks. First contacts/enquiries, providing information, dealing with problems and complaints.

- Scenario-based activities that use the four skills. For example, an assignment for tourism students could include faxing or e-mailing a tourism office to request a map of the town, information on places of interest and a list of hotels and restaurants. The next task would involve ringing a number of hotels and asking about facilities, availability and room rates to suit different budgets. The final task could be a presentation in English about the town and where to stay and eat out, or this could take the form of a report.

Because the outcome of such activities is graded there is scope for recognising individual students' ability and efforts. The ability to be **understood** by a sympathetic native speaker gains more prominence than the traditional requirement for learners to model their speaking output on a native speaker. The tasks also provide a practical application of learning in Key Skills such as Problem Solving, Communication, Information Technology and Application of Number.

A selection of available qualifications

CBLC Certificate in Business Language Competence – OCR

This scheme aims to assess candidates' communicative skills in the target language and can be examined at five levels. At Basic and Survival levels, the assessment takes the form of an oral test. Additionally, a written element can be tested at Survival level. Candidates are given some preparation time before each test to study the Candidate Information Sheet which outlines the task. The oral tests are carried out in the target language, but the candidate may need to demonstrate understanding by taking notes in English (e.g. writing down a spelled-out word or transcribing information). The four skills are assessed at Threshold, Operational and Advanced levels. To obtain a Certificate in Business Language Competence, a set number of elements must be passed for each level. Elements may be taken separately and a certificate listing elements achieved will be issued to recognise achievement if a candidate does not pass or take all elements.

This qualification is gained by passing an externally set test. Centres can select the test date and which elements are to be tested on the visit of the external examiner. Ideally, learners would be tested once they are ready for an element, but this is not practical in terms of costs to the learning establishment and time required.

Example of practice listening tasks at survival level

A department could devise many tasks in English and adapt them for the languages taught.

Sample task	a)	*You are on a plane to Luxembourg.*
		Question: What can you see on each side?
Listen to the		Transcript: You can see France on your right and Belgium on your left.
announcements		
and answer the	b)	*You are at a tube station in Paris.*
questions in		Question: What are you asked to do?
English.		Transcript: The next train is out of service, please wait for the second train.
	c)	*You have asked the way to the main station in Brussels.*
		Question: What instructions did you receive?
		Transcript: Turn left at the end of the street, go straight on and take the third road on your right. The station is at the end of the road, ten minutes away.
	d)	*The following message has been left on your answering machine.*
		Question: Write down the caller's name, company and telephone number.
		Transcript: Hello, this is Mrs Bowan, spelled B-O-W-A-N, from the company Martinshop, spelt M-A-R-T-I-N-S-H-O-P. My phone number is 020 7586 8457. Please call me back.

National Vocational Qualification (NVQ) – City and Guilds and AQA, Edexcel, LCCI, OCR

Originally a vocational award as part of the National Vocational Qualification (NVQ) used to assess competence in the work place or in a simulated environment. The language units are available at Levels 1 to 5 (only to Level 4 with OCR). The assessment of these units is based on a portfolio of evidence and the units can be taken in individual skills (Listening, Speaking, Reading, Writing). The standards for assessment are based on the National Language Standards (LNTO, 2000), determined by the Languages National Training Organisation. The National Language Standards (NLS) provide a national framework for the delivery and assessment of vocational language courses in the context of NVQ. This document defines the language level descriptors at five levels and outlines the elements of competence required for successful completion of assessment in the four skills at each level. The National Language Standards detail the performance criteria that a student must fulfil in order to demonstrate competence in tackling and completing tasks. Students can prove that they can apply what they have been taught by completing tasks designed following the NLS specifications. These specification details are divided into categories covering the four skills (units).

Elements

This section gives an overview of the elements included in the units and information on the performance evidence required. Units are subdivided into elements to make training and assessment of competence more manageable. The performance criteria are listed at the end of each unit.

Assessment guidance

This section provides examples of information to be extracted by the candidate (e.g. personal biographical details, forms of address, social arrangements, common items of personal interest).

Range of use

This section lists the contexts in which the unit should be assessed:

- where and under what circumstances (at work, one-to-one);
- what information is received (common numerical data);
- from what kind of speech information is extracted (simple and commonly used expressions);
- through what channels the user listens (face-to-face, via public announcements).

Underpinning knowledge

Lists the vocabulary and grammatical features that need to be covered, as well as the functions, verification and support and context in which the assessment takes place.

Assessment can be carried out whenever the candidate is ready and indicates this to the assessor. The units are not graded and results are either pass or fail. Although the units can be offered in the sixth form, they are usually used for assessment of a second or third language as they do not qualify for inclusion in an Advanced Vocational Certificate of Education award (AVCE – formerly Advanced GNVQ Language Units; see below) and their UCAS status is still unclear. The NLS provide very detailed information on assessment although the lists can seem daunting if you are used to traditional specifications. Tasks design for teaching and assessment is straightforward because the format is the same for all units.

Example of listening assessment task

Example for Unit L1 (Listening level one): Listen effectively to obtain information about predictable day-to-day activities. This unit is composed of two elements.

- L1.1   Listen effectively for easily recognisable data and facts
- L1.2   Listen effectively for easily recognisable information for action

Performance criteria for L1.1

A competent user at this level can:

- L1.1.1   identify relevant data and facts from simple and commonly used expressions to meet day-to-day requirements
- L1.1.2   in face-to-face situations, acknowledge the speaker politely using appropriate conventions
- L1.1.3   seek clarification and confirmation when needed, using appropriate strategies

Element one (L1.1) can be assessed using a pre-recorded message that will cover the requirements of the first performance criteria (L1.1.1). The task is designed using the assessment guidance to select which examples of information will be included:

- forms of address, greeting, leave-taking;
- job titles, roles, organisation;
- numbers, quantities, price, dates.

A short scenario introduces the task. The scenario and task are in English at lower levels. The message could be recorded in any of the languages taught in the institution adding appropriate names for caller, company and town and changing the phone number and currency. This enables teachers to share resources and reduces their workload as each colleague can work on one unit and devise a scenario and tasks in English that can be translated into other languages.

Example of a task

You work for a company that supplies sports clothes. During your lunch break, a message was left on your voice-mail.

> 'Hello, this is Mrs Smith, Purchasing Manager for the sports shop Move Fast in Manchester. I would like to order 25 black Nike T-shirts in size M @ £10.
> Our client account number is 14 25 63. My telephone number is 0161 236 4159. It is Wednesday 15 February 2001, thank you and goodbye.'

Date

Caller

Company

Telephone number

Customer account number

Order details

Item	Amount	Colour	Unit price

Applied Language Optional Units for use in Advanced Vocational Certificate in Education (AVCE) (formerly Advanced GNVQ Applied Language Units)

At the time of writing, units were offered only by Edexcel.

AVCE programmes are divided in units: six for the Single Award and twelve for the Double Award.

The qualification is available at Levels 2 and 3 (and 1 *ab initio*) and can be taught as integral options within any AVCE programme. There are Standard and Extended Language option units, which can be linked to Levels 2 and 3 of the National Language Standards but have their own assessment criteria. The units focus on either Oral Communication (speaking and listening) or Written Communication (reading and writing) and are designed to be applied to a range of practical situations that relate to the needs and interests of students. Sixty guided learning hours per unit are required. Students studying for the Single Award AVCE (six units) can undertake one language unit and students studying for the Double Award (twelve units) can undertake two language units. The specification states that 'the units primarily focus on the development of practical communication skills, but students should also be exposed to grammatical concepts.'

Grades range from A to E. *Ab initio* units (linked to Level 1 of the NLS) are also available to enable students to develop skills in a new language. The Level 1 units provide a bridge to Level 2 option units but are supplementary to the AVCE main programme of study. The Applied Language Optional Units are assessed internally through portfolios of work. Evidence of achievement includes course folders, audio and possibly video recordings. The board recommends that the qualification is appropriate for students who have achieved a GCSE grade between G and D, a Foundation or an equivalent qualification in the language at Level 2. Those with a GCSE grade between C and A* or Intermediate GNVQ or equivalent are also advised to study at Level 2 or consider Level 3.

The specification contains vocabulary and grammar lists and is divided in four sections:

What you need to learn

Gives information on the types of tasks that candidates will have to achieve and an indication of the vocabulary types in each area.

The tasks for the listening element of the oral communication unit at Level 2 require that the learner 'demonstrates understanding appropriate to different situations through oral or written responses in English (Irish or Welsh) or in the target language'. For the speaking element, 'evidence of the ability to speak effectively in a range of situations and for different purposes' is required.

At the beginning of the course, a possible listening task could consist of reporting orally or writing a memo giving the gist of a recorded telephone message. A speaking task could be to ring a company to order a number of items, giving amounts, colours, prices and delivery address.

The areas are:

- workplace-related language and communication;
- education and training;
- travel and accommodation;
- everyday activities;
- local and international environments;
- non-specific areas;
- situation and settings.

Unit descriptions (by level)

For example for the Oral Communication at Level 2:

* Understanding of the target language in a variety of listening situations.
* Effective communication through target language speaking in different situations.

Assessment evidence

Lists what the candidate should include in his/her portfolio and explains that the work must show the ability to fulfil a number of performance criteria.

Grade descriptors

Grade descriptors for the oral communication unit at Level 2 taken from the Edexcel specifications are as follows:

* Grade E relates to overall student performance which demonstrates adequate understanding and communication skills sufficient for the tasks undertaken.
* Grade C relates to overall student performance which demonstrates good understanding and effective communication skills. The student goes beyond minimal responses and uses a wider range of structures and vocabulary.
* Grade A relates to overall student performance which demonstrates regular examples of thorough understanding and well-developed communication skills. The student uses a wide range of structures and vocabulary, generally performs with confidence and produces mostly accurate language.

NB: The grade descriptors are expanded in the detailed description tables.

Examples of a listening and speaking task at Level 2

This listening task includes a simulated dialogue, it is interactive and asks for information. It also gives explanations and amends an arrangement.

> You had booked two single rooms with bathroom, toilet and television @ ÖS 1,300 but you must process a very important order on the dates you booked. You will have to change the dates of your visit to Salzburg.

<table>
<tr><td>**Task**</td><td>Using the December calendar pages, select a period of four to six days, in case you would like to stay on for the Christmas market at the weekend. Then, ring the hotel to enquire if there is availability on these dates. I shall play the role of the reservation clerk. Make sure to check whether you will incur additional costs.

Do not forget that you can ask for clarification if there is something you do not understand.</td></tr>
</table>

The Applied Language Optional Units provide opportunities to achieve recognition of the student's ability to demonstrate his/her language skills in the relevant vocational context. The Board's performance criteria form the basis for the design of the assessment tasks. The tasks centre on individuals' communication skills.

Advantages of vocational language qualifications

One reason to consider offering vocational languages is that they can appeal to many students who may not have chosen to learn a new language or continue with one examined at GCSE. Vocational qualifications provide accreditation that recognises achievement and enable teachers to deliver courses that are more suited to the practical interests and needs of their students.

* They enable students to continue learning a language beyond GCSE without having to commit themselves to an A level.

* They enable students to learn a new language and provide a qualification even at a basic level.

* They are flexible and allow mixed-ability teaching and assessment.

* They add value to students' portfolio of skills as they provide qualifications recognised by employers and some universities. UCAS is currently reviewing the allocation of points for AVCEs.

Issues

How can these qualifications enhance the motivation of learners?

- They provide instrumental motivation: to enhance work prospects.

- They enable individual target setting.

- Assessment in small chunks is possible.

- They use continuous assessment in class as opposed to test situations (apart from CBLC).

- The learner is in charge of his/her own learning and portfolio and there is promotion of learner autonomy.

- Cross-curricular connection with the core subject makes language learning relevant to the course and offers additional practice of tasks for the core subjects.

- Acquisition of basic knowledge of another language beyond the traditional offer of French and German is possible. For instance, students can obtain a qualification in Japanese, Russian, Cantonese at Levels 1 to 5.

- Tasks are relevant to learners' needs and promote communicative use of language.

- They are nationally recognised qualifications.

What do teachers think of vocational languages?

It is tempting to compare A levels and languages for AVCE because the qualifications reform aims to give parity to qualifications. However, as it does not stipulate a comparable curriculum time for languages it makes a comparison impossible for this subject.

In 1999/2000, CILT surveyed 71 Language Colleges to explore teachers' perceptions of the pros and cons of vocational languages. The results provided the following information:

Professional concerns

Linguistic competence versus task based utilitarian knowledge: A level language students spend four or five hours per week during two years on learning language and culture. The restricted time allocated to vocational languages, often only one hour per week, raises concerns that learners gain a qualification but are not equipped to use the language independently, because it is not possible to teach sufficient grammar and vocabulary and provide adequate practice opportunities during such a short time. Could this mean that the course provides only basic phrases and equips students with methods only to employ the limited amount of knowledge they have acquired? I do not think that the two courses are comparable as A levels appeal to students who are interested in an advanced study of the language, whereas AVCEs appeal to students who want to continue learning the language not to the level required for the A level qualification but in order to use it in practical situations. Teachers were also concerned that where educational provision was led by employers, the aim would be to produce the necessary workforce and dictate which courses were needed, thus reducing choice of subjects.

Practical concerns

The questions relating to whether vocational courses were suitable for the needs of the students and to the types of difficulties and drawbacks teachers were encountering when setting up or teaching on these courses provided information to enable CILT to support teachers through INSET and support materials, e.g. the publication *Qualifications for MFL: Alternatives to GCSE and AS/A level* (CILT, 2000). The following are some of the concerns expressed and suggestions for how to address them.

- Lack of knowledge of the business context. Discussion with colleagues in other departments and reference to teaching manuals will help teachers understand the rest of the course and guide teaching and assessing.

- Teaching vocational languages requires a shift in teachers' view of their role. The facilitator role is increased, while the role of resource provider is less important, as learners are encouraged to use their initiative. Teachers used to academically orientated courses can have difficulties in adapting to these specifications, as the lack of time to deliver the course can lead to teaching set phrases. However, research and learning can be done outside the classroom and students should be encouraged to use self-access resources. They will need guidance on what to use and look out for. Learning contracts are very useful in such a setting.

- Formal teaching does not respond to the practical needs of learners and is not well suited to the task-based learning approach necessary to teach vocational languages. The Boards publish teacher guidance manuals and INSET is also available.

- The 'customer' is different from that on non-vocational courses. Learners might have been de-motivated by a previous negative language learning experience. Additionally, learners might have chosen a vocational path and found that the language module is compulsory although they did not intend to continue learning a language. It is important that learners realise that the course is not a repetition of their GCSE and that the practice and assessment tasks will enable them to apply what they have learnt in other subjects. They need to know what they are going to achieve and how. It is useful to give them copies of the assessment criteria and to explain and illustrate them with practical examples. Guidance on how to organise their portfolio is also necessary right from the beginning.

- Classes tend to be of mixed ability, ranging from beginners to any GCSE grade. The class can be split into ability groups and work on the same theme using differentiated learning materials. Tasks can be assessed at varied levels.

- Lack of resources means that the teacher often has to create them. This adds to the workload. This is unavoidable but there are some commercial vocational resources (see References) and authentic material can be adapted. It is possible to devise generic tasks in English for each module and share them within the department.

- Increased paperwork adds to the workload. Getting used to portfolio cross-referencing can be daunting, but if this is done from the start of the course and you have devised a suitable referencing grid, it will be easy to manage.

- Weighting of skills. The Applied Language Optional Units are separated into: 'Listening and Speaking' and 'Reading and Writing', but it is difficult to isolate each skill. Most courses concentrate on teaching and assessing the Listening and Speaking skills. Reading and Writing skills will still be required as a lot of information comes in written forms, but short reports and news items are increasingly available on the Internet.

- Lack of information. Recent mergers of Boards have led to restructuring. It is difficult to locate staff who can provide information and support. Sample material must be ordered with invoice numbers or paid for in advance. The teacher has to go through layers of bureaucracy beforehand. The school's examination office will take care of this. Teachers need to provide accurate information on what they need. Boards now also make specifications and sample material available on the web (see page preceding Introduction).

- In order to assess your students for NVQ and Applied Language Optional Units, you will need to pass an assessor qualification: D32 and D33; the boards have details of the requirements. This is not necessary for the CBLC.

Conclusion

Although I have stressed that these courses promote learner autonomy because content can be taught and assessed through tasks, I concur with Hughes that 'the fact that candidates are aware that they are in a test situation means that the tasks cannot be really authentic' (1989, p15). Even when learners have the opportunity to be assessed as part of their course, the classroom setting is synonymous with an artificial situation. However, the type of task that they have to complete plays an important part in reducing the artificiality of classroom-based work. Adapting a generic specification to match the needs of learners on vocational courses presents a number of challenges for language teachers. The language course for an AVCE programme may be taught to students on a Leisure and Tourism, Hospitality, Business or Health and Social Care course, whereas the CBLC and NVQs are taught free standing. Borrowing core subject manuals will help teachers to appreciate the kind of tasks (often demanding) that learners have to complete and will provide ideas for language lessons that will be relevant to and useful for the learners. It is also helpful to liaise with the teachers of the core subject in order to be able to mirror in the language class some of the topics that are covered in the other subject. In their core subjects, students will have learnt techniques that they could apply again when dealing with language tasks, thus reinforcing their learning and demonstrating the transfer of their skills.

Being able to teach real beginners' classes will reduce the need to prepare material for different abilities. However, this will often not be possible as learners will have been exposed to at least two of the most commonly taught languages (French, German and Spanish). On the other hand, task-based work enables differentiation as the same tasks can be set but evaluated at different levels. Offering lesser-taught languages can reduce the difficulties associated with teaching a mixed-ability group, but more able learners may come forward wishing to take a higher level certification within the qualification. The CBLC and NVQ qualifications provide accreditation at Levels 1–5 and within the Applied Language Optional Units for use with AVCE, results can be graded from A to E. It should be remembered that learners are not studying the language as an academic subject and the emphasis of the qualifications is on communicative ability rather than grammatical complexity. A further point to take into account is that candidates cannot really fail the NVQ and AVCE assessment because they can be referred for reassessment. Although promoting opportunities, this can have a negative washback on their motivation always to produce work of the highest quality.

Language tests should not contains elements unrelated to language ability (McNamara in Bachman and Palmer, 1996, p96) but learners on a vocational course are accustomed to dealing with work-related tasks as part of their course core units. Students on a Leisure and Tourism course, for example, know the procedure of how to book a hotel room from the initial enquiry to the confirmation stage, unlike most candidates on A level courses who have probably never done so in their native language. They will also have learnt how to deal with problems and complaints.

R. Shohamy called these types of tests: 'performance-communicative task oriented' and condemned them as 'wrong, simplistic and narrow' (1996, p147). For language teachers accustomed to academically oriented courses, adapting to criterion-based assessment is difficult, as this requires being unequivocal about the course objectives. The specifications have been designed to enable students to fulfil tasks that they would be likely to encounter in their professional lives and the assignments can be adapted to enable them to benefit from the demonstration of their ability to fulfil the requirements of the criteria. Therefore, if the tasks fulfil their purpose they cannot be called 'wrong'. Neither is the work 'simplistic and narrow' because the tasks cover a wide range of language and communication ability.

In sixth form and Further Education institutions, funding is largely dependent upon the types of accreditation that students obtain at the end of their course. Decisions about which courses are viable in an environment dependent on income generation are not taken by language teachers. However, beyond their educational value, vocational courses have the advantage of attracting students who might not otherwise have chosen to learn a new language or pursue language studies. The main challenges are to establish these courses within the institution and to become accustomed to a change in delivery and assessment which are task based.

key points

- It is not possible directly to compare A levels and languages for AVCE awards because the allocated curriculum time is different.
- Vocational languages enable learners to apply skills and knowledge acquired in other subjects and to gain a recognised qualification.
- They appeal to students who may not have chosen to learn a language post-16 because they promote learner autonomy.
- Teachers' lack of knowledge of the business context can be overcome by working with colleagues in the relevant departments. Establishing a shared bank of scenarios and tasks in English that can be translated and adapted in the language studied will reduce teachers' workload.
- Assessment is either continuous by means of a portfolio or by tests with an external examiner.

8

Conclusions

There are certainly conclusions that can be drawn from the developments presented in the chapters of this book. But in drawing conclusions from the past, I would certainly not want to fall into the trap of predicting developments in the future! Had I been writing in the 1970s, when there was a pattern of local educational authorities, powerful independent examining boards and when RE was the only compulsory element in the curriculum, I could not even have dreamed of opted-out schools, QCA criteria and the National Curriculum. There is also a sense in which authors predict their own wish list of developments, and I know that my personal wish list is a horse that will fall at the first hurdle. So I claim nothing more for these conclusions than a reasonable interpretation of trends.

It was the Dearing Report which took hold of trends and developments in assessment and gave them a shape and a future pattern. And the word which assaults the eye on reading this seminal report is 'national': 'National Record of Achievement'; 'National Targets'; 'National Certificates'; National Advanced Diploma'. The QCA, first-born child of Dearing, has produced a leaflet on the National Qualifications Framework, and states: 'At the heart of QCA's work is the establishment of a coherent national framework of qualifications, embracing three families of qualification – general, general vocational and vocational, all underpinned by Key Skills.' (www.qca.org.uk). Following the pioneering work of the Languages Lead Body, we now also have the Languages National Training Organisation setting National Language Standards which 'develop occupational standards ... in key activities that are common across a range of business operations.' (www.languagesnto.org.uk). It may not be evident to more recent arrivals on the scene, whether in teaching or testing, but this profligate use of the adjective 'national' is actually quite neologistic in the English educational context. It certainly establishes a trend, which we can now reasonably assume to be unstoppable. Dearing referred to the range of qualifications for 16–19 year olds as 'vast … at least 16,000'. A major purpose of his review was to bring order into this apparent anarchy, hence national standards and the rest. Of course, this means the loss of some corners of individualism and free enterprise, but in the context of examinations, the movement also brings greater fairness, transparency, accountability and a wider understanding of how results are reached.

So, one conclusion we can reasonably draw is that the process of increasing rationalisation, centralisation and uniformity traced in this book will continue. The National Framework of Qualifications, drawn up by Dearing (1996, p13) and refined by QCA (see below) will remain an important template for further developments:

Examples of qualifications in the National Framework

Level of qualification	General	Vocationally-related	Occupational
5 Professional	Postgraduate⁺	Higher level qualifications⁺	Level 5 NVQ
4 Higher	Honours degree⁺	Higher level qualifications⁺	Level 4 NVQ
3 Advanced level	A level	Vocational A level (Advanced Vocational Certificate of Education)	Level 3 NVQ
2 Intermediate level	GCSE grade A*–C	Intermediate GNVQ	Level 2 NVQ
1 Foundation level	GCSE grades D–G	Foundation GNVQ	Level 1 NVQ
Entry level	Certificate of (Educational) Achievement	Certificate of (Educational) Achievement	Certificate of (Educational) Achievement

⁺ *Responsibility shared with the QAA (Quality Assurance Agency) for Higher Education.*

We can expect an increasing drawing towards the centre of all the many strands which have so far characterised examination and assessment in England and Wales. The question which cannot yet be answered by a general observer is whether the days of the Examination Boards as independent operators are numbered. The inescapable logic of the process is that a National Examinations

Board should eventually emerge. Already criteria are laid down nationally and Board syllabus specifications have to be approved and vetted. Within England there now exist only three Boards exercising the functions of myriad bodies that existed a short while ago. It would be a short step indeed for the Boards to become administering agencies of a national board.

If that is one trend which can be detected without great perspicacity, the other is contained within the QCA statement quoted earlier, claiming that it embraced 'three families of qualification – general, general vocational and vocational, all underpinned by Key Skills.' This implies a reference to a major problem of the whole assessment system, the lack of parity between 'academic' and vocational qualifications. The problem is not unique to the UK. France, for example, aimed to change perceptions by changing nomenclature, and gave the name *Lycée Professionnel* to what had been *Collège d'Enseignement Technique* and developed a range of technical and vocational examinations under the prestigious *Baccalauréat* title, such as *Baccalauréat Technique* and *Baccalauréat Professionnel*. In the same way, the clearly formulated pattern of Dearing's National Framework grants parity in name and status. The next step is to make that status actual and to change long-standing attitudes. It is hard to see that the differing aims and concerns of vocational examinations (see Chapter 7) could lead to a common exam that would have any meaning. But parity of esteem is certainly desirable and possible, for there is ample evidence that perceptions can be changed. Factors such as the equal availability of such qualifications, the ease of switching between courses and the attitudes of employers and Higher Education could well lead to genuine parity between qualifications in the National Framework.

One further development, relevant to high-achieving students, may be referred to here. Part of the remit of QCA is to develop 'world-class tests' which would ensure that the levels demanded of the highest-achieving students 'are tested against standards comparable with the most demanding to be found in other countries.' This is the Advanced Extension Award, currently being piloted in French. The AEA is targeted at the top 10% of students at A level. The aim is 'to stretch the most able A level students by providing opportunities ... to demonstrate greater depth of understanding than required at A level'.

A level has addressed an ever-wider audience as post-16 education has expanded and more students aspire to Higher Education. The spectrum of ability now evident in the field of post-16 education requires a different approach from the past; not a narrowly academic approach, but demanding courses whose final qualifications are appropriate to the individual students, whether those qualifications have an academic or a vocational bias. But there is clearly a sense that doing justice to the whole spectrum of talents and ability may still require something more to filter out academic ability at the highest level. That is the purpose of the Advanced Extension Award.

In reviewing the developments in assessment of Modern Foreign Languages over the past 25 years, there are certainly causes for rejoicing and also, as in all change, reasons for regret. One can rejoice at the increased range of skills tested and the relevance and immediacy of the language now taught. But one might regret the marginalisation of the literary and creative element which once formed the backbone of A level language courses. What cannot be denied is the astonishing flexibility of a system which has been able to absorb such changes of philosophy and direction. And one can only admire those classroom teachers who have echoed that flexibility and shown themselves, for the good of their students, constantly able to adapt to the world of teaching and testing languages as that world changes around them.

References

Bachman L and A Palmer, *Language testing in practice* (OUP, 1996)

Bialystok E, *Communication strategies* (Basil Blackwell, 1990)

Carroll B J, *Testing communicative performance* (Pergamon, 1980)

Curriculum 2000 (QCA, 1999)

Davies A, 'Language testing: Survey articles 1 and 2' in *Teaching and linguistics abstracts 11:* 145–59 and 215–31 (1978)

Ellis G and B Sinclair, *Learning to learn English* (CUP, 1989)

Gaskell R, 'Using foreign texts in post O-level teaching' in *Audio-visual language journal,* Vol XV, 1: 26–35 (1977)

Harrison A, *A language testing handbook* (Macmillan, 1983)

Hawkins E, *Awareness of language: An introduction* (CUP, 1984)

HMSO, *Foreign languages Key Stage 3, first year, 1992–3* (1993)

Hughes A, *Testing for language teachers* (CUP, 1989)

Jones B, Advanced Pathfinder 2: *Developing learning strategies* (CILT, 2001)

Lewkowicz J A, 'Authenticity in language testing: some outstanding questions' in *Language testing,* Vol 17, 1: 43–64 (2000)

Lussier D, '*Evaluation et approche communicative*' in Monnerie-Goarin A and R Lescure, *Evaluations et certifications en langue étrangère* (1993)

McCulloch D, 'Where has all the grammar gone?' in *German teaching* 12 (ALL, December 1995)

McKeon J, *Language portfolios for students of language NVQ units: Tutor's guide* (CILT, 1998)

McLachlan A, Advanced Pathfinder 1: *Advancing oral skills* (CILT, 2001)

The National Language Standards 2000 (The Languages National Training Organisation, 2000)

National statistics: Social trends (HMSO, 2000)

Neather E J *et al, Target language testing in Modern Foreign Languages* (SCAA, 1995)

Nuffield Foundation, *Languages: The next generation* (Oxford, 2000)

SCAA, *Review of qualifications for 16–19 year olds* (The Dearing Report) (1996)

Schools Council, *New patterns in sixth form modern language studies,* Schools Council Working Paper 28 (Evans/Methuen, 1970)

Shohamy E in Brown G, K Malmkjaer and J Williams, *Performance and competence in second language acquisition* (CUP, 1996)

Widdowson H G, *Teaching language as communication* (OUP, 1978)

Websites

Languages National Training Organisation: www.languagesnto.org.uk

Qualifications and Curriculum Authority: www.qca.org.uk

General vocational information

CILT information sheets are available on-line on the CLT home page at www.cilt.org.uk/info0.htm and provide lists of vocational teaching materials for:
- Business and vocational French (sheet 62), German (sheet 63) and Spanish (sheet 64)
- Sheet 24 provides a list of publishers and distributors of materials for language teachers
- Sheet 25 provides a list of bookshops and sources of supply for language teaching materials

The CILT publication *Qualifications for MFL: Alternatives to GCSE and AS/A level* is available on-line at www.cilt.org.uk/qualifications/index.htm

Applied Language Optional Units for use in AVCE: Guide to unit specifications. Specification no: G006 765 (Edexcel, 2000)

OCR publishes free 'Information briefs' for the Certificate in Business Language Competence. Publication order line: 0870 870 6622. Fax: 0870 870 6621. E-mail: publications@ocr.org.uk

A list of alternative accreditation including a summary of each qualification and contact details for the Examination Boards is available on-line at www.cilt.org.uk/ qualifications/index.htm